WHERE CAN I FIND MRS GASKELL?

WHERE CAN I FIND MRS GASKELL?

(Diary of a Hay-on-Wye bookseller)

KEITH GOWEN

Keith Gowen

GOMER PRESS
LLANDYSUL
1985

First Edition—July 1985

ISBN 0 86383 134 6

© Keith Gowen

*Printed by J. D. Lewis and Sons Ltd., Gomer Press,
Llandysul, Dyfed.*

To Mary

ACKNOWLEDGEMENTS

I would like to thank Dr. Roger Ellis of University College, Cardiff for reading the manuscript and for his many helpful suggestions. My thanks are also due to Mrs. Vicki Press who brought order out of chaos to the final typescript.

CONTENTS

ILLUSTRATIONS

Cover illustration by Mary Parker

Illustrations by Andrew Gowen

FOREWORD

Hay-on-Wye eighteen years ago was a quiet Welsh border town at the foot of the Black Mountains. Visitors came to fish in the River Wye which skirts the town, to commence a trek along the path of the ancient Offa's Dyke or to purchase a Welsh pony at the local pony auction. Hay in those days had a cinema, a fire station, a work-house and a very large furniture emporium known as ''The Limited''. But one day the cinema ceased to function as a picture house and instead became filled, top to bottom, with second-hand books— thousands of them. Then the fire station fell, once more to books, and the work-house stopped taking in the elderly, only to become the last resting ground for ancient theological works. Sometime later ''The Limited'' gave up selling furniture and turned its attention to selling yet more books. And so it was that Hay became choc-a-block with second-hand books. One couldn't move for them, until eventually the pressure on space was so great that the weightier of the dusty tomes were offered to the public as a substitute fuel for wood-burning stoves. The founder and propagator of this new industry was Richard Booth, a former Oxford undergraduate and local boy. It is to him that Hay now owes its fame as the town known throughout the book world as the ''town of books''.

Since those formative days in the '60s, books by the ton have passed through Hay to be distributed in the various shops that have sprung up, and now the very name of Hay is inseparably linked with Richard Booth and the second-hand book trade. Except for books, there is no earthly reason why the town should receive such attention. There are no main roads passing through the place. It doesn't lead to anywhere in particular. Still they come: the reporters from the Wall Street Journal, The Times and Le Monde; television crews from Belgium, Germany, America and many other countries; above all, the lover of books. But how much longer will these seekers after news and learning and a good read continue to traipse down country roads in order to put in the obligatory attendance in the ''town of books''?

Some have come and gone with a keen disappointment at what Hay has had to offer and murmurs of disillusionment are afoot. How long can Hay go on commanding this world-wide acclaim? One thing is for sure; it can no longer rest on its laurels and benefit from past fame. Its days of adulation and attention are numbered if it ceases to offer the book connoisseur and the book lover something worthwhile.

In the midst of this bookish scene, standing opposite the OXFAM shop in St. John's Place and just up the road from the Wheatsheaf Inn and the ancient hall of St. John's Church, stands the Arvona Gallery. Twelve years ago Arvona was a Georgian town house of some dilapidation. Now renovated, the property houses, on the ground floor, an art gallery and bookshop. Arvona Gallery has been maintained by the writer from his home in the Vale of Glamorgan, which has entailed a weekly journey over the Brecon Beacons, often in the most atrocious weather. The journeys have been undertaken to the accompaniment of fog, frost, wind, rain and snow and sometimes, when the passage has been at its most perilous, the writer has called into question the wisdom of running such a distant operation, particularly when the gallery has been deserted. But it is in moments such as these, when the television crews, newspaper reporters and, most importantly of all, the book seekers have departed and left the town to its own devices, that there has been the opportunity for him to sit down and quietly reflect on the lonely lot of a bookseller. Out of this has emerged the following diary.

There have been times in his Hay sojourn when the tin-opener has been at its most active, and thus all the inadequate and amusing self-caring has gone into the record as well. But the personal heartsearchings as to why he remains in the town through thick and thin are banished when there steps across the threshold of the gallery some interesting person who gives meaning and purpose to the whole operation. Loyalties receive a new lease of life and the "town of books" once more exercises its unique fascination.

"I never travel without my diary. One should always have something sensational to read in the train". Oscar Wilde

1984
January 8th (Sunday)

I have just returned from the usual sojourn up at Hay. It was one of those slightly uneasy week-ends with rumours of the weather getting colder. Since we were trapped in the Brecon Beacons three years ago I have always been edgy whenever there is a prediction of snow, particularly when alone. I have visions of becoming trapped indoors without food and slowly starving to death. Hourly I have a panic buy in Havards and usually come back laden with tins of this and that. Then I re-think my position "is this going to be sufficient in an emergency?" and over I go again for another lot until Mrs. Havard is beginning to suspect my strange behaviour. The panic buying goes on throughout the day until there are stacked in the kitchen long lines of soup (always the Heinz variety), loaves of bread, mashed potatoes in packets and custard tarts. At the end of the day I am ready for any crisis but the snow never comes and I am left having to finish this lot off before leaving for home. Take this morning for instance. After cornflakes, I had to get down to heated-up noodle soup left over from the night before. Noodle soup at nine in the morning—yuk!

Of course, if it came to the push, I console myself with the thought that Havards is just over the road. In a nation-wide snow-up, I visualise headlines in the Sun—'DESPERATE GALLERY OWNER HACKS HIS WAY INTO LOCAL FOOD-STORE'. Well, I know it sounds far-fetched, but in a life or death situation I wouldn't hesitate to do just that!

I have to admit, living on one's own, if only for a few days, does make one realise the lot of old people. What would happen for instance if I fell down stairs or failed to get out of bed? I have toyed with the idea of having a brick by my side, which in a situation of extreme immobility could be hurled through the window bearing a message 'HELP, I AM IN BED ON THE FIRST FLOOR'.

1

Then there is the ritual of turning off the water supply before the 60-mile trek for home. This is a major plumbing and engineering job. I am the world's leading authority on stop-cocks! I know precisely where they are. I know exactly by how much pressure they have to be squeezed and I can even accomplish all this in the dark unaided. It gives me the most enormous sense of well-being to leave for home knowing there isn't a drop of running water in the house. The snag is when I return the following week and have to turn them all on again. The house vibrates as if it were some Heath Robinson machine and water rushes joyously through the pipes like a great waterfall! It's no wonder with all these threatened traumas around me that I go to the Blue Boar to escape. But the troubles do not end there. Last Saturday night I left the pub in such a state that half-way down the road the dreaded thought came upon me that I had locked the keys in the house and that I wasn't going to be able to get in. Newspaper headlines once again flashed across the mind—'GALLERY OWNER FOUND FROZEN TO DEATH ON DOORSTEP'. In a state of panic, with hands deep down in trouser pockets, "I think I have lost my keys", shouted I to an acquaintance who happened to be passing by. Knowing from whence I came, he suggested I "might have left them on the table". At that precise moment and on the same side of the pavement up came Geoffrey Aspin to my rescue who reassured me that if I was to end up in the gutter, locked out of house and home, he would put me up for the night. This gave me confidence to propel myself back home and, praise be, there were the keys to the house in the glove compartment of the car. So I have now developed a new fetish—keys!

The other Hay phobia I have acquired is that of a hair cut. I only have to cross the road for a trim and usually I book myself in with Jill as her first customer of the morning. The snag is that Jill is a workaholic and it is nothing for her to be seen working away at seven in the morning. Many times I have woken and glimpsed the shadow of Jill reflected in the bedroom window as she has gone about her hairy tasks. And not only that. I sometimes wake with the thought that I have overslept for my hair-cut. As a result I now lie awake all night for fear of being late. This Saturday morning was no

2

exception. I went to the salon and said to her, ''You don't know what I have gone through to keep this appointment.'' She is a good, cheery young soul and laughs it off but if only she knew the sacrifices I have made so that she may pass her fingers through my silken hair!

January 9th (Monday)

I have at last had a display cabinet delivered to the gallery, specially made to measure by a local carpenter. It measures some eight feet long, four feet wide and four feet high and has been built to display pictures and prints on a flat top with a deep well at one end in which unframed prints can be stood and examined. Directly underneath the well are two storage drawers with flaps for the inspection of smaller prints. The display top has been very cleverly designed so that it can be lifted up to enable large frames to be hidden away in the unused space underneath. So far so good. But the moment I saw the contraption being unloaded off the roof of the van, I knew we were exposing ourselves to ridicule and the thing began to metamorphasise before my very eyes! When the display top was lifted to reveal the dark spaces beneath, it immediately became apparent that it could comfortably sleep two people. The well at one end of the unit took on the appearance of a pulpit and the two hatch back drawers below, instead of containing small elegant prints, housed rabbits and racing pigeons! In this sort of situation the best one can do is to face up to the reaction of the public head on and I am thinking of putting a notice over the two hatch-back drawers to read 'Please do not feed the animals'.

The creator of this contraption is a splendid fellow but unfortunately accident-prone. I was warned by a colleague in Hay who some weeks earlier had had the unfortunate experience of losing one of his plate glass windows when the carpenter was at work. I had completely forgotten the warning until one day he was doing something to a door in the gallery which leads into the office. He was vigorously slamming the door to and fro to see if it would ride comfortably over a

3

carpet, when suddenly he shouted—"look out!" I just caught sight of a picture flashing past my right ear as it fell off the wall and came crashing to the ground at my feet; it was only then I remembered my friend's enquiry—"Have you had any accidents yet?"

From my flat window last evening I saw something which moved me very much. It was a young woman toiling over a hot stove baking cakes for her little tea shop. There she was, with an air of slight indifference reading off a piece of paper, probably checking to see that she had the oven at the right temperature. She was bending down to put this in and take that out. It looked an exceedingly tiresome task for that time of night. And then I reflected that she cannot be doing that for fun, she probably has to earn a bit extra. This morning I made a point of passing her little shop to see if anybody had taken an interest in her labours of the night before. There were still a lot of her cakes unsold. I wonder how she felt? Perhaps I should have bought some myself.

I have recently had a letter published in the December issue of the *Antiquarian Book Monthly Review*. I was bemoaning the fact that Richard Booth and his latest arrival and rival at Hay seem to attract all sorts of free publicity for themselves and their enterprises whereas I never receive a mention. I could display a Turner watercolour in the gallery window for £10, I complained, and still the press and public would walk straight past. Not even wearing a city suit or walking the street with uncombed hair had attracted the least attention to myself or the gallery. Well, from past experience, I should have known better than write to the press. For instance, I remember on one occasion in my teens I wrote to a National newspaper over a rather spiky Archbishop of Wales and was promptly invited by a crank in the Outer Hebrides to join their monastic order. Then there was the time when I complained bitterly in the letters column of the *Western Mail* at the British invasion of Suez and nearly divided myself off from my father as he read my piece with acute embarrassment over the breakfast table.

But on this occasion I did get a sensible response from someone in Cheshire who wrote to tell me that if I only opened the gallery more frequently then my plaintive cry

4

The Clock Tower

would be answered. He was quite right and hit the nail on the head. Only weeks before I had taken a small step to publicise the gallery. I am a poor one for Christmas decorations and find they make the place look untidy. But this year I was determined we were going to put on a show. We bought all of £1.69 worth of streamers and bells from a D.I.Y. centre in Merthyr and before anybody else had had a chance to set their shop windows ablaze with bunting, there was the Arvona Gallery looking like a rear window of Harrods. (A very rear window). We displayed all the right books, poems and pictures for the Christmas season. All that remained now was to stand back and wait for the shoppers to pour in. "Thank-you," said a little boy from across the road as he watched us perilously fixing tinsel to drawing pins. We needn't have bothered. Nobody came in; but we did have the satisfaction of being festive. We will know better next time.

January 15th (Sunday)

Somehow I don't think that lady in the cake shop could have quite made it. I heard this morning that her tiny premises have been sold and they are planning to turn it into a wine and bistro bar. We might never again see her seed cake and apple pies and plum tarts. What a shame.

This week-end we had the first real threat of snow. Ever since we became trapped on the Beacons three years ago and had to take refuge in the Storey Arms in a raging blizzard, I have always viewed the journey from Cowbridge to Hay and back in winter with some trepidation. I set out from home fully prepared for all eventualities. Sleeping bag, a flask of hot homemade tomato soup, extra clothing, a torch, a spade —all stowed away in the car. The only items I didn't carry were rockets and flares! But nothing happened. I arrived in Hay on the Thursday evening quite safely and arrived back home again on Sunday quite safely.

For all the customers I had, I needn't have bothered with the trip. Three people came into the gallery throughout the week-end and one of those was not stable. There he stood in the doorway and announced in a loud voice—"Have you any books on Cornish pasties and Devonshire clotted cream?" He made this enquiry as if he had just sampled a few there and then, for the words came out of a moistured mouth. I timidly made some excuse for not having any and responded that I didn't think many books had been published on such mouth-watering topics, to which he replied, "Oh, I've got nine 'undred of 'em at 'ome." It was then that I realized we were not twelve to the dozen and began to feel uneasy in his presence. If I had been quicker on the uptake, what I should have said to his enquiry was "No, I am sorry I haven't anything on Cornish pasties and Devonshire clotted cream but I am expecting a fresh supply in on Monday!" But as always happens on these occasions, a witty response is never on hand.

January 20th (Friday)

Today has been another one of those days when I am convinced I am never going to sell anything again. Hay is windswept and deserted and not a soul has entered the gallery. I might not have bothered to put up the 'Open' sign. But it is on days such as these that you can really get on with the work without chit-chat and interruption, and I have managed to get a lot of jobs done, which is some compensation for the lack of sales.

January 21st (Saturday)

Went down to open the gallery first thing this morning and outside the door of the flat and on the white boundary wall there was blood spattered. Pools lay on the floor and long, congealed trickles were everywhere. I didn't hear a fracas in the night and how it got there I shall never know.

It was almost as bizarre as a conversation I overheard at the Blue Boar this evening. A few of us were having a drink to celebrate the opening of a new bookshop in town and I was only half tuned in to what was being said. I could hardly believe my ears. It seemed that a person at our table was actually offering to purchase the head of the person sitting opposite when he departed this life. A lot of haggling went on until at last a price was agreed and a cheque crossed the table for £25. At first I thought I had been drinking too much but gradually it dawned on me that they were deadly serious about the whole macabre business. I was able to confirm that this strange conversation took place with two other friends who were also witnesses to the event.

One of the party was Jerome. He is an habitual punner but on this occasion I think I did get the better of him. He was telling us of a report in a newspaper that day of a collector of old violins who had taken his box of tricks to a firm of well known auctioneers. The box contained bits and pieces but the unusual thing was none of it had been glued together. When the auctioneers, however, had sold this serendipity it was discovered that many of the parts did in fact go to make up a rare Italian violin of the 17th century. Jerome wondered why the owner of this little lot hadn't gone along earlier to an authority and found out what it was all about before the auction. "Well Jerome," I replied, "he hadn't the guts to go and ask anybody." For just once, Jerome was stumped for words!

This afternoon I had a visit from another one of the wits of Hay: Michael Cottrell, better known to everyone as Cotters. Cotters is always comparing himself to some rare exotic South American bird. As a professional bookseller he will wander around the gallery trying to find an elusive bargain and when he tires will exclaim in the lightest of voices "I feel like an Oriental Flying Gunard" or some such other exotic creature. I know what's coming, and for months I have been trying to think up a description of myself which would at least match in exoticism Cotter's description of himself. Predictably out came the anticipated expression from my visitor to which I countered, "Well, Cotters, I feel like a 14th Century Burmese wind instrument." And as I said it, I thought to myself 'beat that'.

In spite of all this light-hearted banter between friends, it has been a strange week-end, what with the sighting of blood in the early morning and the bartering of a head in the late evening.

January 28th (Saturday)

One of the advantages of having a desk in the window is being able to hear exactly what is going on in the road outside. I often tune in to all sorts of weird conversations and usually get advance warning of what is about to enter. I heard one such between man and wife this morning. From what I could make out, they had just made the startling discovery that I sold pictures and one was trying to persuade the other to venture across the threshold to show me something. "Go on Bert, look, he's sitting there doing nothing, he won't mind," I heard her say. Eventually after much peering they both plucked up courage and jointly confronted me in the doorway of the gallery. There they stood, thunderstruck, looking down at me and then at the pictures on the wall behind. I seemed to be some strange creature and they became completely tongue-tied. After standing with mouths open for an embarrassingly long time, the wife finally managed to pose at least half the question—"Do you sell"—she said—"do you sell"—all the time leaning forward pointing to the pictures. The word just would not come! Finally, her powers of description completely failed her and she stood with her husband gazing at me in suspended animation. "What do you call those things on the wall behind 'im?" she asked the bewildered man, to which he replied "Pictures, love." "Yes, that's it," she said triumphantly—"do you sell pictures?" I could hardly say no when I was surrounded with them. She then asked if she could bring some in to see if I might be interested in buying. After much to-ing and fro-ing from a car, the couple produced their treasures. As they were laid out in front of me for inspection, they looked for all the world like rolled-up strips of linoleum. The first masterpiece was some sort of oil-o-graph of a country scene in the style of Wolworth's circa 1949 with a hole in the middle! This was quickly followed by other works in descending order of merit, ending with a the pièce de résistance of the collection

9

—a weeping Madonna. The trouble was, she was weeping tears of blood! "Are you interested?" asked the lady tentatively. I have been through situations like this before and have learnt to handle them with a certain amount of diplomacy. I declined with the tactful explanation that the articles were not really the sort of things I sold in the gallery. But still they persisted and still I refused to buy until the husband, more in desperation than anything else, resignedly capitulated with the comment—"I suppose they are for the rubbish dump then, are they?" For just once, I threw all caution to the wind and delivered the brutal and final answer, "Yes." With that they departed and went on their way perfectly happy.

February 4th (Saturday)

I am about to poison half the population of Hay, which on Hay's past criminal history is nothing unusual! This will be brought about with six potatoes, 1lb of cheap mutton, two onions, 2oz mushrooms, one kidney, and a quarter pound of mushroom stalks. I shall mix the whole lot together in a saucepan, call it Lancashire Hot-pot and invite my friends around for the feast.

I have never done this sort of thing before; in fact, I am just about capable of boiling an egg. But this morning, after taking one look at all the tins of this, that and the other that I have opened this week-end, I decided for health reasons I must learn to cook. It stands to reason that with all the artificial colourings that go into tins these days, it can't be doing me any good eating this sort of food. I really must get something more substantial inside me.

Katharine Whitehorn, in her little cookery book for beginners, tells me that I should start with a Lancashire Hot-pot. I therefore intend making a start. I am certainly not going to eat this on my own and have specially selected some of my closest friends to come along to act as guinea pigs. They have been chosen for their strong constitutions and with luck we should get by without anyone collapsing on the floor with stomach pains!

10

Today has been another one of those dreadfully still, silent days in Hay when nothing much seems to happen. I have been busy in the gallery preparing to take to auction some of the stock which has been hanging around for a long time. Then after that, moving things from one place to another. Whether it makes any difference to the sales I very much doubt, although to the outside world I must appear very busy. Peter Smith, who is a local friend of mine, came in half way through the morning for a chat and a warm and told me of the walnut dumplings that he makes. They sound absolutely delicious and I am sure I am going to get an invite from him one of these says; meantime, it was up to the Blue Boar at lunchtime for the usual pint and onion soup. Chris's onion soup is a meal in itself; unfortunately, it gives me the most enormous bouts of wind. Lunches at the Blue Boar these days become more and more prolonged and on the way back I have to call in Geoffrey Aspin's shop as a port of refuge to sort myself out. The visit usually ends up with roars of laughter and now I think they expect me as a matter of course so as to bring some cheer and merriment to their day. Geoffrey was really in need of cheering up today because he has had such a bad week for sales, even though his shop is situated in a prime site in the High Street.

Many of the booksellers of Hay and others who have come to the town to escape from surburbia would class themselves as the Alternative Society, but in these dormant days of Autumn and Winter, with nothing much to do and nobody around to sell to, the question is to find an alternative to the Alternative Society. The idea is to make enough money in the high Summer months to see one through the Winter and most people do precisely this. But I still cannot help asking myself, what on earth can one do between November and March in this forsaken town? I suppose if I had the patience I should set to producing a couple of really first class catalogues and try selling off a mailing list. Producing one or two good catalogues is time-consuming enough. Alternatively, there is the temptation to escape to sunnier climes. I think I should plump for this idea. Perhaps one day I shall have the courage to carry out my convictions.

Until that day arrives, the occasional Winter visit to the Auctioneers must suffice. We did that today, Monday, 6th February, when we decided to put some stock into Jollys of Bath. For a start one needs three A levels to find a way around the one-way traffic system of Bath and a certificate in advanced motoring when the Auction Rooms are finally discovered. The trouble doesn't end there because you next have to find a parking space. We thought we had found one, until half-way through the auction it was announced, "Would the owner of car MWO 181X please return to his vehicle as it is causing an obstruction?" We immediately returned to our offending child to be told that only five minutes earlier four strapping undertakers had been grappling to manoeuvre a coffin over the bonnet of the car. I hadn't the faintest idea we were parked directly outside a funeral parlour but the man who told us was awfully nice about it as we drove off into the February rain. I think we had better think of escaping to some sunnier climate after all.

February 15th (Wednesday)

I had a telephone call today from my good friend, Stephen Bainbridge, of Ludlow. When business is slack at his end I usually have a call from him to go and buy, and invariably I come away with something good. He has a remarkable ability to create a sale. If trade is bad he will get out on the road and put together a selling opportunity. It is a gift to be able to do this. I am a poor salesman and find it difficult to put across with conviction any faith in the article I am selling. My attitude is, "Well here it is, have it if you want it." Stephen has the hallmarks of a professional, which I do not possess.

We first met when Stephen had a bookshop in an out-of-the-way town in mid-Wales called Knighton. I wonder how many people could say where Knighton is? Since our first meeting we have had many memorable buying trips together, mainly in his car. To experience Stephen driving is an event in itself. I do not recommend it to the faint-hearted.

My first trip with him was to North Wales. On the way back we became mixed up in a motor rally and sandwiched ourselves in between the leading cars in the race. On we sped into the night. By the time we reached Bala at eleven o'clock we were being wildly cheered by spectators who had lined the route under the mistaken impression that we were in the lead. It was only when we stopped for chips that we managed to disentangle ourselves from an extremely embarrassing and unnerving situation.

I finally retired from the Stephen Bainbridge Book-Buying Rallies last year. That was after having hurtled along the winding lanes of the Golden Valley on the way back from Monmouth to Hay. I had a sick headache; I wanted to spend a penny; I was mentally and physically exhausted with the tension. When it ended and I was ejected outside the gallery, with quivering lips and shaking knees, I handed in my resignation there and then—at least until the next time.

February 16th (Thursday)

One of the facts that is becoming abundantly clear to me is that in these dark Winter days one can expect to do very little business. Previously I had looked at Hay through rose-tinted spectacles; the town could do no wrong, never mind what time of the year it was. Now I have altered my ideas and doubt very much whether it is worth heating, lighting and manning a gallery for a non-existent public.

I wasn't aware that this other side of Hay existed until I tried coming up on a Thursday instead of my normal Friday night, which has been my pattern for the past ten years. This has meant that I have been seen walking around the town at unfamiliar times and has led to total confusion in the minds of the locals. Seeing me on a Friday morning, the populace automatically assume it is a Saturday. Only now are the older members of the community getting the hang of my movements and realising what day of the week it is. Some are in such confusion as to be beyond recall.

13

Opening time at The Blue Boar

I thought perhaps there would be more life up at the Blue Boar tonight than there was in the gallery. There were only six of us around Chris's welcoming open hearth fire.

February 17th (Friday)

Tonight, however, was a very different story. The pub was so crowded that I was unable to occupy my usual place in the settle, which usually houses four regulars. Now there is a very strict order of seniority as to who sits in the settle. First and foremost there is Jim I who holds the dual role of Father of the House and Speaker and nobody ever sits in Jim I's place. Should a person be foolish enough to try it, he would be like a tourist sitting on the Woolsack. The next in order of precedence is Jim II. Jim II is a life-long friend and companion of Jim I; a quiet and efficient deputy he is too and almost as regular a settle settler as his senior. Sitting in at week-ends is Jim III who is a Hay boy born and bred and who loyally returns home whenever he can. Finally, bringing up the rear, there is me, who although a comparative outsider has joined and enjoyed the three Jim's company over the years.

But on this night, the almost unheard-of actually happened. Someone was sitting in Jim II's place in the settle. Now Jim II doesn't command the respect of the House in quite the same was as Jim I or this wouldn't have happened. But there he was—stood—actually stood at the bar. I sensed there was something dreadfully wrong the moment I walked in through the swing doors. Jim II's eyes were restless as they flashed from his glass to his familiar place in the settle. Jim II is usually a placid man but tonight there was fire in his eyes.

Eventually, the poor hapless and totally innocent settle pincher went his way and normality was restored. Perhaps it isn't a bad thing to play occasionally at musical chairs.

February 25th (Saturday)

I said farewell today to my good friend and former partner, Peter Dance. Peter and I were brought together by accident

15

some twelve years ago through our interest in English water-colours, and we have been firm friends ever since. Peter moved to Hay in 1972 and I followed in his footsteps to set up in partnership with him in my existing premises under the partnership name of Arvona Gallery. I owe a great deal to Peter for it was he who opened many doors for me, particularly to the world of books. I recall how, when we used to enthuse over the joys of collecting watercolours, Peter would say, "Ah, but you wait 'till you start collecting books." Little did I realize at the time what this would mean and how much it would alter the course of my life. From that moment I started to take a serious interest in book collecting—to such an extent that it has now very nearly displaced my first love. Picture selling can be a very slow, silent process: now that the gallery has been converted to sell 50% books, the turn-over is greater and, more importantly, much more satisfying. Books have a human feel about them and speak of ideas.

I have been able to pursue my business career but this has also meant that my time in the gallery has been restricted to week-ends. Peter on the other hand threw everything to the wind twelve years ago when he decided to leave the cosy confines of a safe museum life and has lived off his writing and entrepreneurial skills ever since. I admire him for his courage in giving up a secure job in order to live a life of his own choosing.

In 1981 we amicably agreed to terminate the partnership and go our separate ways.

He and Una have decided to live in Spain. Strange that on the very day they announced their intentions of living abroad and thus starting a new life, I too should tell them that I was starting out on a new life also; for today I terminated a business career—after 38 years.

March 3rd (Saturday)

My God—it's snowing, and I am up here on my own. Whatever am I going to do? I must go over to Havards and start getting in some emergency rations.

It is also falling-down-holes day. Hay at the moment resembles Ypres in the First World War with craters all over the place. If you are not careful you are likely to fall into one of these gaping holes and end up with either a man from the Electricity Board, the Gas Board or the Water Board or all three. I have been trying to sort out poetry books but with all this din going on how on earth can one turn the mind to higher things? I don't think I am ever going to sell anything again. Reg Coombes cheered me up no end this morning as I panic-bought at Havards. He said I looked a City gent. For months now I have tried to be noticed but the trouble with this place is that they all dress so scruffily, the only chance one has of standing out is by wearing something terribly orthodox like a suit or a tie. Well, I have tried a suit, a natty tie, even a pair of Barkers buckled shoes (which cost me a fortune); but nobody ever takes a blind bit of notice. I then went to the other extreme, of not combing my hair or putting my dentures in, but with the same dispiriting result. Then suddenly I hit upon a brilliant idea. What about a Crombie overcoat and a silk scarf partly concealing a casually unbuttoned shirt with a rolled-up umbrella? Surely it would be worth a try. It worked like a dream. Ever since I got myself up in this ensemble people have been stopping me in the street and saying how interesting I appear. Cotters says I look like a figure out of the Decadent 90's which pleases me immensely. Richard Booth says I look a City accountant and Stephen Bainbridge simply said I was "dishy"! But my days of sartorial elegance must surely be numbered. After all, how can I go around the town in flaming June dressed in a Crombie overcoat and swinging a rolled-up umbrella?

I might get away with the umbrella, because that stops me from falling over, but surely not an overcoat, in mid-Summer. I may have to resort to one of those nice striped shirts with a neatly pressed stiff white collar and matching tie and cufflinks. Yes, that might work.

Chris Fry, landlord of the Blue Boar, was in one of his best coarse moods today. He invited some woman to come and stand in front of the fire to dry her knickers out.

The author with Jim I

March 10th (Saturday)

I have just bought a whole run of modern first editions. Graham Greene's 'Our man in Havana', Ian Fleming's 'From Russia with Love', John Steinbeck's 'Sweet Thursday', 'Mountolive' by Durrell, 'Venus Rising from the Sea' by Bennett, along with many more by authors such as Tolkien, Graves, Wells, Wodehouse and so on. This is a new departure for me because in the past I have tended to slavishly follow fashion and mainly buy those books that it was claimed everybody else wanted, which I suppose makes commercial common sense if nothing else. Books on natural history were all the range a couple of years ago, as indeed were those on topography, particularly the plate books, which dealers knew but wouldn't readily admit were broken up and the plates mounted and framed as pictures. If a Roscoe's Tour of Wales came one's way you felt you had to snap it up and the price rose as consistently as the F.T. share index. But I had the feeling, their days were numbered, it was being over-done, and sure enough the market fell away. Admittedly, I still have some remnants of those books in the gallery even now, and the plates do make attractive pictures for the Summer visitor. There remains a market for this type of book at a more realistic price level. I began to realise, however, that there was more to book collecting than the attraction of coloured plates. Looking back now I also suspect that my choice of books for the gallery partly reflected my own prefer-ence. All my life I have been in the habit of reading books because I have felt them to be 'good' for me. I remember as a lad wading through Homer and potted biograophies of the World's great philosophers when I would probably have enjoyed myself just as much reading a William book. I envy my wife who can become so lost in a 'good' book that she is oblivious to all that is going on around her. With me it is quite different. The more I try to concentrate, the more I become distracted by outside influences. ''What boring book are you reading now?'' she will ask me as I try to anaesthetize myself against the outside wold. ''Ah,'' I retort, ''but it's educational.'' I yearn for a good read for its own sake. And so it was that when I came upon this collection of first editions,

I saw my chance to change course. Here was an opportunity to get lost in something for no other reason than it was absorbing. So I bought the lot. I thought at first they would make a change in the gallery but instead I brought them home! Hemmingway is good; perhaps when I get to Graham Greene I will have achieved a state of Nirvana.

We get some extremely curious people passing the gallery these days. One such sight is that of a man who passes up the road every Saturday morning. His trousers are so short they end where the lower part of the shin begins. One is never quite sure whether he is wearing long shorts or short longs!

We are going to have to rearrange the seating at the Blue Boar for the next couple of weeks because Jim II has just announced that he is going to work in Daventry and will only be coming home at week-ends. Jim III is staying at Bournville for the next two weeks and I am off to Amsterdam next week-end which means that Jim I is going to be on his own. This is an extremely grave state of affairs but I am quite confident that Jim I will pull through without us all.

I am also pleased to be able to report that with the arrival of the young and attractive Mimie in the kitchen of the Blue Boar, we have at last had a change in the soup course. So that when Mimie came forth with her delicious carrot and orange soup a great many people in Hay breathed a sigh of relief.

A friend confessed this afternoon that because of the difficulty in making ends meet, he has had to give up taking *The Times*. So times are hard. This was the last thing he thought he would ever have to do because he had been a *Times* reader since he was a lad of fifteen. This sad news came from one of the best read men I know.

AMSTERDAM

Amsterdam has come and gone for the sixth year running and I am as fond of this city now as when I first discovered it. I managed to time my visit on this occasion to be there for the European Antiquarian Book Fair which was interesting, but fairly low key. The main purpose of my trip, however, was to call on Wout Vuyk who has a bookshop in Spuistraat 316. It was in his shop that I put my feet up, on an earlier visit to Amsterdam when we drank tea together and consoled ourselves on the state of the book trade. Ever since then we have been good friends. One has to be careful reaching out for the elusive volume in Wout's shop. The careless removal of a book from a four foot pile could bring the lot crashing down on the customer. By the very nature of the architecture, Dutch shops are not easy to get around, and so it is that in Wout's premises an intricate system of passing signs has to be employed by browsers in order to facilitate the unhampered progress from one part to the other. In narrow passageways it is fascinating to see what ingenious signals can be employed between one customer and another. In the process I have had many interesting conversations with total strangers. Parked bicycles used to be another hazard; often I have had to disentangle protruding bits of clothing from handlebars and brake wires (but the offending machines have now found other parking grounds.) As with so many bookshops, the quiet working away at a seam of books in remote parts can produce the most bizarre effect on the countenance and often I have walked away from a stock pile looking more like a Black and White Minstrel than anything else. Whilst on the subject, I think a short Act of Parliament ought to be brought in banning all bottom shelves. Wout's shop still bears all the hallmarks of being a genuine browser's bookshop and all credit to him for that. But improvements are afoot which will make it much easier for the free passage of customers of whom there is a quiet trickle throughout the day. The English bookman might be hard pressed to find the English book, for the shop caters first and foremost for the Dutch collector, but there is always a friendly welcome and who knows what one may find?

Just off Spuistraat and in the adjacent Voorburgwal 304 is to be found Mr. Emmering, specialising in prints and art books, and a few hundred yards further down the road, Mr. Israels. Also in Voorburgwal 284 Mr. Johannes Marcus has his art gallery displaying Dutch paintings; he also carries a stock of English topographical prints and art reference books.

Further afield in Spiegelgracht 8 and on the way down from the Rijksmuseum, Mr. J. v. Brink has a gallery devoted mainly to 20th century graphics; he also has a splendid selection of modern art reference books.

It was in another part of the city that I very nearly became grossly misunderstood. I went into a shop which I thought sold very attractive glass pipes. But on closer inspection of the goods on display and in particular of a book which offered me advice on how to grow cannabis under artificial light, it gradually dawned on me what it was all about. I became so carried away with the novelty of the experience that I quite forgot where I was and where I was straying and it was only when an assitant drew my attention to the fact—"You are behind the counter Sir,"—that I took it into my head to flee as quickly as possible.

On Friday evening we went to the Concertgebouw for a concert given by the Concertgebouw Orchestra of Amsterdam with Antal Dorati conducting. There is something distinguished and venerable about this famous concert hall, which was built towards the end of the 19th century. Its foursquare structure and plain classical simplicity always remind me of a very large non-Conformist chapel rather than a World-famous concert hall. In fact, its Protestant exterior is very much in keeping with its plain unadorned interior, with a large encircling balcony adorned with plaques commemorating famous composers and conductors who have appeared in the hall in the past. Come to think of it, a large pulpit in the centre wouldn't be at all out of place. The members of the Orchestra make their entrance from stage level whereas the conductor descends from on high down a long length of carpeted stairs in full view of the audience and it takes all of thirty seconds to make the precarious descent to the conductor's rostrum. One false step and the poor man could have the most calamitous fall in front of 2,000 people, which according to Wout has been known to happen. The only other comparison I can think of which approximates to this unusual procedure is that of English professional cricketers and their amateur captains of years ago. The players made their entrance on to the pitch from one part of the pavilion followed by the captain descending a separate flight of steps from another part of the same pavilion. The Protestant analagy doesn't end there either because I have the impression that when the Dutchman has a night out in the Concertgebouw it really is a Sunday-best-suit occasion. But for all its formality, music-making at this wonderful hall can be a memorable experience. I remember as a boy many years ago buying a record of the Concertgebouw Orchestra under van Beinum, who was their conductor at the time. The sound that struck me then was the wonderfully unique lush tone of the string section and, sure enough, there it was again on Friday evening.

I did manage to get around the City fairly well under my own steam with the aid of the rolled-up umbrella but I still find one of the great dangers for the pedestrian in Amsterdam is of being run over not by a bus but by a bicycle. The riders swoop in packs or in pairs, but by far the most lethal is the lone rider with the enormous wheels who steal upon the unsuspecting, silently and stealthily, in narrow alleyways. Here there is no chance. He performs with the utmost dexterity, sometimes with one hand, sometimes with none, and more often than not with a passenger perched on the back wheel. Saturday is a very busy day for the cyclist in Amsterdam. Lots of shopping has to be done and a common sight is the potted plant being cycled home. I cannot speak Dutch but I am proud of the fact that I can pronounce Concertgebouw fluently. In fact, I think if I was flattened by one of these machines and I lay there expiring in the road, one of the first things I would try and do would be to utter the word CONCERTGEBOUW. The pronounciation would be so impeccable that they would rush me off to hospital under the impression I was a Dutchman. But what do they do with these machines when they have to leave them? By far the most popular parking places are lamp-posts or on bridges over the canals; here you see them tethered in their thousands. It is not always easy to say how long some of these machines have been deposited by their owners. Some have been there for only a matter of hours whereas others appear to have been parked in their present resting place for hundreds of years, often looking abandoned and forlorn like one I saw this morning with all the signs of rigor mortis; so much so,

23

that only the front wheel remained, still securely fastened to the lamp-post.

Visits to Amsterdam make one wish the aerosol can had never been invented. The ugly messages of graffiti are sprayed everywhere, defacing this lovely city. They drip from the walls of public buildings and even from the seats of buses and trams. Surprisingly, one of the few public buildings in the city which has not come in for this sort of treatment, and which one would have thought a prime target, is the now empty Royal Palace in Dam Square. In the square this evening was a lone Scottish piper in full regalia, playing or blowing Amazing Grace with a biting Easterly wind blowing straight up his kilt. At his feet there was a collecting box inscribed "Thank you" in five languages. Even Scottish airs played on the bagpipes must be better than the banal message of the aerosol can.

Any person who has witnessed my walking will know that fleetness of foot is not one of my strong points and my lack of agility certainly let me down on this latest trip to Amsterdam. One afternoon after a great deal of walking I decided that I was badly in need of a coffee to revive my flagging spirits and a coffee shop quite near to Spuistraat seemed to be an ideal place to pop in to. Pop in to is perhaps not quite the most appropriate choice of words on this occasion—jump in to would be a better description. For this is exactly what I was called upon to do by a floor layer, who had just reached the crucial part of his work and was about to affix four new steps of tiles in the doorway when I arrived. He had completed the spreading on of a thick coating of a glutinous tar-like substance and was about to place the floor tiles into position. Taking one look at me standing there he barked out the command "Jump" from his lava-flowing floor, meaning that I should take one enormous leap, thus clearing in a bound the four steps that lay before me. Looking back now, with the benefit of hindsight, I realise I should never have attempted it. At the best of times it is bad enough for me to walk up steps, let alone leap up them, but on this occasion my sporting vanity got the better of me and on the command "Jump!" I set off. The moment my right leg shot out in front of me

I knew I was doomed to failure. There was no conceivable way I was going to be able to clear the four steps. I think the floor layer too must have sensed an impending catastrophe, because half-way through my antics he shouted at the top of his voice "NO." It was too late; I had taken off. There was no way I could turn back. I landed with a dull plop right in the middle of the liquid tile fixer. He was already in a kneeling position when I landed and like something out of a Tom and Jerry cartoon, I squelched past him and made my sticky passage down the shop to order the coffee, leaving a trail of Hush Puppy prints behind me on the newly laid floor. He was very good about it, and by the time I was ready to leave the shop I was relieved to see that the floor tiles on the steps had been hurriedly laid. I dread to think what would have happened if they hadn't been.

On the afternoon of my return home, Wout kindly went out on his bike and brought back armfuls of tulips for Mary. And so it was that I returned to Wales with tulips as the sole remembrance of my trip to Amsterdam with not even a duty free bottle of scotch to be seen anywhere; in fact, this could have been my downfall. The Customs Officers do not like to see travellers passing through their net with no duty free and they immediately become suspicious when one proceeds to do just this. "No duty free, Sir?" I was asked incredulously as I stood with a heavy weighted suitcase. "No," I replied. "Open up your case, would you, Sir?" he requested, probably thinking he was on to a very good thing. Now there is nothing that gives one greater satisfaction and a feeling of confidence than passing through Customs with a completely free conscience. Therefore, it was in a spirit of bravado that I opened up my treasures to the all-suspecting eye only to reveal first editions of Tolkien, Huxley, Henry James and so forth. All these had been plucked from the bookshelves at a great price; the price of life and limb I mean, but what a disappointment for the Customs man.

March 24th (Saturday)

After Amsterdam it is something of an anti-climax sitting here in the gallery waiting for the customers. The 'Open' signs have been put up, the heating switched on and the gallery is ablaze with electric light, but it doesn't make a scrap of difference. Here we are at the end of March and Hay is still as silent and deserted as ever it was in mid Winter. Are we ever going to change this place? I begin to wonder whether it is all worth it. Why bother to present the stock in some sort of decent order? Come to think of it, why bother to get in a large new stock at all if the public is not around to see it? And I convey my thoughts to Mary, and I think even she senses that I am not far off becoming disillusioned with the town of Hay, after all these years of faithfulness on my part. But wait a minute. At about eleven o'clock the door is pushed open and in walk Tim and Stella from Fulham. Tim and his wife have been good customers of mine in the past, and I haven't seen them for months. Granted, they haven't come in to buy anything today but simply to say hello and have a chat. Then, shortly after that, Peter Smith makes his morning call, soon followed by Fay and Sheila whom I met last Summer for the first time. I shared an evening meal with them at the cottage where they were staying. Fay has just successfully obtained her BA Degree with the Open University and the two girls beamed with delight to be back in Hay. Soon the gallery is a hub of conversation and laughter and it is just like old times again. This is the infuriating thing about Hay. Just when you are at your lowest and even toying with the idea of packing the whole enterprise up, somebody or something will turn up out of the blue which alters your whole attitude to the town. Today has been no exception. Somehow I seem to have acquired the reputation of being a friendly chap running a friendly gallery, and this has made many new friends for me; ample compensation for all the disappointments past and present.

26

March 30th (Friday)

Tonight I had dinner with Peter Smith in his book-lined flat overlooking Clyro and the glory of his collection is that he has actually read all these books. Peter doesn't collect for the sake of collecting, but quotes from books with relish and out of a sheer love of literature. The walnut dumplings were delicious.

I took along my new Rameau record of the religious motets; we played them but didn't listen to a note, because we talked so much. It was a delightful evening, and now it is up to me to show what I can do with my cooking. I thought I might try out my Lancashire Hotpot on him (I still haven't got around to concocting it)—so here is my opportunity.

March 31st (Saturday)

It is an absolutely bitingly cold day in Hay, so much so that people are walking around the town complaining of headaches because of the wind blowing on their exposed heads. The peaks of the Black Mountains are covered with a sprinkling of fine snow, and it is going to take a great deal to tempt visitors out on a day like this. Late March and early April can be deceptively treacherous months of the year, just when you think Winter has passed, and today is no exception.

At lunchtime I made my usual Saturday mid-day call on the Cinema Bookshop and went straight to Greg's office, which is a bookshop within a bookshop. The Cinema has three or four such inner sancta, which normally house a better class of book and are relics of the days when Richard Booth used to own the Cinema. They usually hold out hope of finding something new of quality and access to them is either by request at the desk in the foyer or by asking one of the staff who happen to be on duty at the time. It so happened Greg was in his office on this particular morning. He apologised to me for the terrible smell. I thought at first

The author with Peter Smith about to set out for the walnut dumplings

it was moth balls but the longer I stood rummaging among the shelves the more conscious I became of something stronger and certainly much more acrid. It was in fact the smell of a decomposing mouse who in a Rentokil raid on the premises had taken it in to its head to pass away under the floorboards. The Cinema people had been reluctant to take up all the floorboards and this camphor-like substance had been scattered around the room in a vain hope of putting down the mousey smell, but with no very successful results. In the end, the stench was so strong, books or no books, I had to come out.

Although tomorrow is April Fool's Day, today is that strange phenomenon in Hay which Richard Booth calls Independence Day, and marks the 7th Anniversary when Richard declared UDI for the town and proclaimed himself King of Hay. Since then the world's press has been taken in by this eccentric gesture. When it was talked about some years ago, to many of us it seemed no more than a schoolboy prank, and certainly not witty enough even to be classed as undergraduate humour. But it caught on, and the media have never ceased publicising such a dotty idea. From Paris to Pretoria, they have descended on the town. Richard Booth and Hay, "the town of books", have featured in every periodical from Punch to the Wall Street Journal, and television crews from as far apart as America and Austria have all been here. Today has been no exception. This time it has been the turn of Belgian television. They have infiltrated every conceivable corner of Hay with their arc lights and microphones. The locals are as hardened to this sort of attention as if they were residents of Hollywood. I make one exception to this: a certain Mr. Bell who works in the bookshop called "The Limited", which represents the last great bastion of the Booth Empire at the other end of town. "The Limited" was once a huge, rambling furniture showroom which flourished in Hay's more orthodox days. Now it houses vast rows of bookshelves and the poor, unwitting Mr. Bell, was deputed by Richard to take charge of the Belgian television crew and act as their interpreter when they arrived to film. This was because Mr. Bell confessed to "having a slight commercial knowledge of French''; at least it was sufficient to get by when he was selling machines in Paris. There he stood on this bleak Saturday afternoon, with not a soul in whispering distance to offer him encouragement, awaiting the cameras and film crew with all their paraphernalia, trembling at the knees for fear of being asked anything awkward in French. ''Richard asked if I could speak French,'' said the hapless Mr. Bell—''but this is bloody ridiculous.'' I didn't have the heart to tell him the broadcast was going out to Belgium, France, Germany and Switzerland with him acting as the official interpreter! I think that would have been too much for him!

In the evening we all traipsed over to the castle for the Independence Day banquet (to that part which still has a roof over its head). As I stumbled in the pitch dark in the grounds over broken planks of wood, fallen masonry and empty buckets, the thought went through my mind how very useful these television people would have been with their arc lights to guide us to our destination. But they were inside filming the celebrations. There was a three-piece folk group to film, the locals, some very nice visitors from Belgium, and a little trendy group who had taken a lot of time and trouble to make themselves look untidy. Finally King Richard emerged from what looked like a pantry, robed in a gown and cape, carrying an orb and sceptre, his shirt hanging out at the back.

It was a gloriously disorganised occasion which only Richard can put on and get away with. If I or some of my more orthodox friends had attempted such a venture, we would not even have been laughed at but simply ignored. But he has this unique flair for publicity for which Hay must be indebted. I would go further and say that the second-hand book trade owes him much for having brushed away the dust that has for so long settled on this esoteric trade. Over the past years, through my business connections, I have had to spend some of my time at receptions, business lunches and dinners. Whenever the conversation has lagged and I have been stumped for something to say, invariably the mention of Hay-on-Wye evokes a response. ''Ah,'' will come the reply

—"isn't that where Richard Booth has all those second-hand books?" (for the two are synonymous). Richard has his faults, but the world of books in general, and Hay-on-Wye in particular, would be a duller place without him.

April 7th (Saturday)

We have been in Hay since early Thursday afternoon, but I am afraid the Blue Boar has seen little of me. This is partly due to Peter Smith having had an evening meal with me on Thursday. It wasn't the guinea pig run that I had been planning to try out on him for so long, but a quick 'knock-you-up meal' which my wife prepared and through which we talked incessantly. When it was over there was no time for the Blue Boar.

I did manage a visit on Friday evening and was struck by the number of unhappy people who seem to be in Hay these days. I couldn't help over-hearing some of the conversations taking place, and it really was a revelation. I have thought of Hay as the ultimate escape route for people in search of an alternative way of life from the pressurised society in which we live but I wonder, if in fact, they have found what they are searching for. Making ends meet is a struggle, and I am now beginning to question whether the struggle is proving too much for some of them. On the other hand, I know of one person who has never been happier and is living off the most meagre of pensions. I suppose if one has the creative capacity to get the most out of life, some of the possessions, which we consider so vital, are not important at all.

Turning away from the more serious aspect of life, today I had one of those slightly odd experiences which make life so amusing. Half-way through the morning a charming man came in who had the manner of someone who was earnestly seeking something or somebody and in the kindliest way enquired—"Where can I find Mrs. Gaskell?". Standing in front of this slightly stooping figure, I racked my brain as to who Mrs. Gaskell could possibly be—she certainly wasn't known to me. As the caller held his ground, glancing first to his right and then to his left, and finally imploringly at me, I eventually blurted out—"Does she work for OXFAM opposite?" "No,"—he replied—"Mrs. Gaskell, the biographer of Charlotte Brontë." Exactly the same thing happened down in The Limited. To the enquiry "Is Mrs. Gaskell upstairs?" the girl at the desk replied, "I haven't seen anyone going through here"!! I will simply add as a footnote to the whole embarrassing episode that I was able to supply him with two of the three Mrs. Gaskells he was seeking.

But this hasn't entirely been a day for light-hearted banter and jollifications such as we had the week before; rather there is a tension running through the town which I think most people sense. I had an inkling that something was wrong yesterday afternoon when I had a call from a person totally unknown to me who said he was from Booth's asking if I would call to see him in the 'Limited' that afternoon. One hasn't to be particularly perceptive to realise that when a request of this kind is made there is something afoot. I made my way down to the 'Limited' but after waiting in a side office for some ten minutes, it became clear they were all so busy in meetings on the premises they didn't really have the time to see me. So I will never know what the request was about.

VENICE AND THE GREEK ISLANDS

April 11th (Wednesday)

At last we have been able to get away from Hay and are about to set out to see something of the world. We have decided to go on a Swan Hellenic cruise to Greece and the Greek Islands. As we stand here in rain-drenched Venice waiting to board our cruise ship, which will be our home for the next fortnight, I can't help reflecting, as I look around our fellow passengers, that we are enlising with retired generals, old ladies, the elderly infirm. (I have cause to withdraw unreservedly the last comment, because I discovered as the voyage progressed that most of these people were indeed lively and delightful.)

As I glance up at the ship's rail from the quay, I see some of the crew eyeing us from the boat deck observing the talent about to embark. I have a feeling they are going to have to do some sharing because there is precious little talent about. That is with the exception of one attractive young lady who is standing at my side and I venture my first remark of the cruise—"It's all up to you, you're carrying the flag." Judging from her laugh, I think she knows exactly what I mean.

Who would have thought that Venice was to be the testing ground for my newly acquired plastic mac? But here we are in the pouring rain looking like drowned rats waiting to board the ship. Not far away I notice agile Venetians jumping into tiny, bobbing bus boats in the gusty rain. If some of the elderly about to go aboard our ship were called upon to perform this aquatic, acrobatic act, they would probably jump straight into the water.

The sight of so many of us on the quayside is reminiscent of sheep dog trials, the high spot of the exercise being reached when the shepherd coaxes the poor dumb animals into the pen. Baahing and bleating we make our way to the safety of our cabins.

"Oh dear," there are no coat hangers for the suits and evening wear we have brought. An urgent message is despatched to Kostas, our cabin steward, who promises action in "two Greek minutes". His prompt attention bodes well for the rest of the voyage.

Boat drill is, of course, obligatory on board and as we sail down the Adriatic past Venice, we are summoned on deck to be informed what has to be done in the event of an emergency. Life jackets are donned in the cabins and the sight of some three hundred human beings of all shapes and sizes, inflated beyond recognition, lurching down alleyways and up staircases, is a sight to behold. For fifteen minutes we stand shivering in serried ranks in the order in which we have been commanded to assemble. i.e. women and children first, but in our case, as there are no children, it is women and old women followed by men. There falls a silence while the

33

officials endeavour to make up their minds whether or not the ship is sinking, followed by gesticulating and whistles of the crew. Then it ends and we are dismissed. The drawback of an exercise of this kind is that folk haven't had time to acquaint themselves with the geography of the ship. Consequently, passengers have not the faintest idea who they are, where they are, and how to get back to where they have just come from. The effect is that for some considerable time after the boat has ''sunk'', elderly ladies are seen wandering around the vessel in inflatables seeking to find the way back to their cabins. Indeed, some are found later that evening in a confused and bewildered state.

April 12th (Thursday) AT SEA

I am now beginning to appreciate the value of that boat drill the night before, because we have just sailed into the most atrocious weather. All was calm until we went to bed last night but no sooner had we put our heads down on the pillow than the ship began to pitch and roll, and by day-break it was clear we were in the teeth of a force eight storm. Our cabin is on the third deck, but the waves are such that the spray reaches to the porthole. With the arrival of daybreak we mistakenly assume the situation is improving. In the event we give both breakfast and lunch a miss. All we can do is to lie on our bunks and wait patiently for the storm to abate.

By mid-afternoon, just when the storm is at its worst and we are all laid low, over the ship's tannoy comes the beautifully soothing voice of Professor Stanford to deliver the first of his lectures on Ancient Greek history. How the man can remain upright, keep a clear head, and give us the benefit of his wonderfully lucid thoughts, is a miracle. The effect he has on the troubled mind has something of a biblical quality about it. Well, that is classical training for you. I gather this opening lecture was addressed to the entire ship's passengers as they lay in their sick beds!

At 16.00 hours Kostas, the cabin steward, came around to check that we were still alive and to bathe our bed sores! I was well enough to lift my head from the pillow to receive at the

34

hands of Mary, in sacramental fashion, a sea sick tablet! She was in fine fettle and able to journey to the dining room for a couple of tiny ship's biscuits. By now there were clusters of passengers in the lounge, albeit huddled in corners with heads cupped in hands. At 20.00 hours it was possible to stand, dress and even keep some dinner down. About half the passengers were well enough to follow suit and some were even able to make coherent conversation.

So ends our first twenty four hours at sea.

April 13th (Friday) OLYMPIA

When we went to bed last night we were silently hoping and praying that the storms we encountered on sailing from Venice were behind us: but that was not to be. We have just spent another storm-tossed night, having during the small hours gone to the rescue of a fishing boat that had got into difficulties. So with the storms and that little diversion during the night, our arrival at Katakolo today has been delayed. The consequence of this is that our fellow passengers are still wandering around the ship looking slightly shaky and seedy and not a few, as a result of sea-sickness, are temporarily widowed. But by mid-day most of us are feeling sufficiently confident and well to venture up on deck and lounge around in deck chairs, taking in the fresh air.

After a buffet lunch on board, we were herded off to the first of our many excursions on Greek soil, a visit to the ancient site of Olympia. I use the word "herded" to describe what we must have looked like as we were shepherded from ship to coach, coach to site, site to museum, museum to coach, and finally coach back to the ship. Some gambolled all over the place like new born lambs. Others strayed and had to be shooed into line. Finally there were the stragglers, usually the photographers, who were so weighed down with the paraphernalia and impedimenta of modern photography it was a wonder they were able to stand, let alone walk.

The site of Olympia, bathed in the Spring sunshine, was one of tranquility and stillness. Standing on what was once the racing track of the first Olympic runners, it was difficult to project the mind forward to today's Olympic scene with all its razamataz and petty politics. Our Greek guides spoke of the dispute that is at present taking place between the permanent Olympic authorities and the Los Angeles committee (where this year's games will take place) as to the commercial exploitation of the Olympic torch, which will be kindled on this very site and carried symbolically to the New World. Our toes explored the stone starting blocks which steadied and then propelled those early athletes down the track that lay before us. Today's youths to our right, raced up and down the sacred earth for sheer joy and to be able to tell their folk that they too had sprinted up the first Olympic track. Today's modern Games seemed far removed from the localised scene before us.

By evening we were all back on board for the Gala Dinner and judging from the chatter going on around us, it was clear that all thought of the storms of the previous two nights were firmly at the back of peoples' minds. Or were they? I have a strong suspicion they were not. Deep down inside, folk were still a little apprehensive as to what lay ahead and the way they talked of early disembarkations which were to come, revealed much of what they were really thinking on perusing their schedule for the following day. Their line of reasoning went something like this. For the first two days of this trip we have been roused from our slumbers by the tossing of a wind-swept ship. Therefore, it follows as normal practice, that for the first three hours every day we are going to be sea-sick. But no allowance has been made for this by the Swan people. Instead, they talk of an 8.00 hours disembarkation, "So how the hell can I be sea-sick and at the same time get through a bacon and egg breakfast, shipped into a bobbing motor launch, transported twenty miles by coach and be on site by 9.00 hours. I can't be expected to be ill and acting the part of a tourist at the same time. I have to have sufficient time for each."

That, I am convinced is how some were feeling, and if Swans on their daily cruise programme had allocated ''6.30 hours to 8.30 hours sea-sick time'' many naive people would have believed them. It took a lot to reassure some that by early next day they would be sailing into becalmed waters. This was the burden passengers took to bed with them as they entered their third night at sea.

April 14 (Saturday) DELPHI

We needen't have worried too much about ropes down alley-ways, sea-sick tablets, or jamming bottoms between bath-room door and wash-basin to remain upright, for at last we have sailed into calmer waters.

Today we visited Delphi. The site of Delphi lies at the foot of two great crags of Mt. Parnassus and here Apollo was born and the will of the god was interpreted by the first Pythia; a venerated woman of Delphi who through the inhalation of the earth's vapour became clairvoyant and predicted the future. Men came from all over the ancient Greek world to consult the oracle at Delphi and to learn of the prospects for their enterprises both great and small.

For us mortals it rained at Delphi. Instead of being able to view at leisure the Temple of Apollo, the Sacred Way, the Theatre, the Treasury and all the other considerable ruins, we were reduced to long columns of moving plastic tents as we snaked our way around the ancient site. Steaming mack-intoshes, colourful umbrellas and chattering humanity on the way up to the Temple were met by identical groups as they slipped and slithered on their way down from the Temple. In this atmosphere, it was difficult to imagine that here was the very place where men from all over the ancient Greek world assembled to have their fates foretold. How difficult it might have been reconciling the guide books with what actually lay before us. But Delphi triumphed. As the rain was wiped away from sodden faces, it still was not unreasonable to imagine that this place was indeed the home of the gods, and from here they lived and moved and had their being. Delphi, even in the rain, was a place of great mystery, grace and beauty; feminine in the same way as Venice is fem-inine. If the gods dwelt on Earth it was surely here. What must Delphi be like in the white light of the Greek sunshine?

THROUGH THE CORINTH CANAL

April 15th (Sunday)

We are now into the fourth day of the cruise, and it is interesting to observe how passengers are beginning to unbend towards one another and utter thoughts they would not have dreamed of expressing earlier. The restaurant at dinner is ample proof of this, judging by the hubbub compared to the polite silence of the first night. The only problem is the impossibility of being able to hear, let alone understand, what the person directly opposite is saying: there are times when the only point of coherent contact I have with a fellow diner occurs when I see his or her lips moving up and down. The result is that there have been moments when I have gone off on a tangent which has turned out to be totally unrelated to what has just been said—which is very embarrassing. So out of dire necessity, I am sure there are people on this cruise who are learning to lip read very quickly.

Faces too become familiar due to the confined space in which we move around and which makes it impossible to avoid one another. For instance, I keep meeting an American lady who wears some sort of trinket around her neck which looks for all the world like a frying pan. The ornament is so large and weighty and has such jagged ends that I am sure if she were to fall on it, it would inflict the most fearsome damage to her person. Then there is the gentleman who has become inseparable from his civil service brief case. Whether he is lounging in the sun on deck or scrambling over some ancient ruin, there he is with the crown jewels firmly attached to himself. I wonder what he does carry in that diplomatic bag? Perhaps they are the deeds of his house. Another passenger I am constantly bumping into is a man whose sole physical activity seems to be embroidery. Be it after dinner in the lounge or upon deck, out come the needle and thread and away he goes. Whatever he is constructing, is certainly very colourful.

During the late hours of last evening we made the silent passage through the Corinth Canal, a four-mile stretch of waterway that separates Western Greece from Eastern

Greece and shortens the journey from Athens to the West by 200 miles. The transit takes about forty-five minutes. Relying on the power from an escorting tug, we all find the journey through the central section, with a 300 foot deep cutting in the sandstone rock on either side, an eerie and claustrophobic experience.

At the other end of the canal, we once more encountered bad weather, so much so that we had to abandon a planned visit to Skyros to visit the tomb of Rupert Brooke. It was impossible to land. Instead we sailed on to Skiathos where once more we made a late arrival owing to the weather. All in all, things are not going too well for the cruise directors, and the unscheduled minor disasters that have occurred on this voyage read like some minor Greek tragedy. This is a catalogue of the unexpected events that have taken place so far. Bad weather on sailing from Venice, involving a diversion to pick up fishermen in difficulties. Hasty retreats from Delphi in torrential rain. Abandoned visit to Skyros and a late arrival at Skiathos. Finally, strikes on mainland Greece of museum staff which have required a hasty re-arrangement of schedules. This afternoon the cruise director actually used the word 'jinx' in issuing her amended battle orders for the day, and we do sympathise with her. The staff are battling on manfully, much to their credit.

Sitting in the lounge this morning, not quite knowing what is happening or where we are going next, one of the lecturers looked at me rather forlornly and said, ''You know, there are people on this ship who do not have the faintest idea where they are, and oughtn't to be here at all'': and as we lurched on to our next port of call, I can quite understand why. Coffee on these occasions is a great soother. As passengers struggle to keep their balance and not spill the cups, they all look slightly tipsy.

Eventually we arrive at Skiathos in the late afternoon sunshine and as the ship does not berth alongside I know what is going to happen. We are going to be taken ashore in little boats, and then off again, in Dunkirk fashion. And as sure as eggs, the passengers are going to make a bee line for the shops. With that prospect in mind, we both stay on board and catch up on some much need sunbathing. Rumour has it that we are in for another stormy night, but I haven't the heart to break this news to the returning shoppers.

April 16th (Monday) TROY—'STONE, BONE AND COPPER THINGS'

We have now sailed through the Dardanelles and we are in Turkey and at one of the famous sites of the Ancient World. Troy. Troy is a place hidden in legend and the mists of time but is brought to life again by Professor Stanford, as he stands on the city walls and recites in the ancient Greek tongue one of the epic poems. Troy lay hidden from modern man until it was un-earthed by the energetic excavations of a German, Heinrich Schliemann in the 1870's. Since then it has become a place of pilgrimage for all who are interested in classical antiquity.

Troy is not just one city but nine, and in times past each successive city has been built one on top of the other. We had already been warned in advance of the damage Schliemann had inflicted upon the site as a result of the unscientific way he had gone about excavating the area. He dug through everything, in the same way a child would carelessly demolish a sand-castle and here it was for all to see. Untidy pile upon pile, making it difficult to identiy one ancient site from another, all bearing testimony to the frantic way in which Schliemann and his team had gone about uncovering the cities of Troy. He was seeking King Priam's treasure, and, sure enough, there in one corner of the site is the very place where Schliemann is said to have made the discovery. In that respect he was supremely successful. As an archaeologist though he must have been a problem. One hasn't to be trained to realize the haphazard way he went about his task and to see the damage caused. Surely an ancient site would not be tackled in this fashion today. I found it ironical to reflect that an American archaeological team actually had to excavate one of Schliemann's own mounds!

Considering the importance of Troy to the Ancient World, the site appears to be surprisingly parochial, covering an area of perhaps not more than a few acres. It reminded me very much of a North American Heritage Museum. There for instance was the incongruous Horse of Troy, constructed out of wood five years ago, standing sentinel at the entrance of the car park! The museum too was quaintly homespun, with its corrugated iron roof adjacent to what looked like the village stores selling cheap souvenirs. The museum contained one endearing inscription attached to a cabinet housing some of the priceless treasures of Troy, which read ''stone, bone and copper things'' and that to the uninitiated typified Troy.

April 17th (Tuesday) TURKEY

Overnight we have sailed from Troy in the North to Bodrum in the South of Turkey. An award ought to be made to the Maritime Archaeological Museum and Castle at Bodrum for being one of the most attractive and interesting museums along the Ionian coast.

From Bodrum we drove northwards to Ephesus. It is during the course of this journey that one is forcibly reminded that Turkey is a very different country from Greece. The physical characteristics are striking. Greece is part of Europe, Turkey is the last segment of Asia and the meeting point between East and West. The journey through the countryside recalled the familiar biblical words ''and there were shepherds in the fields abiding . . .'': the country people we saw seem to have stepped out of a Poussin landscape. A lone boy tending a dozen sheep under the olive trees in a meadow bedecked with the lovely wild flowers of the area; further on a herdsman and solitary cow, together reclining in a timeless landscape, one in harmony with the other and both in total harmony with nature. Probably the cow has seen as much of the world as her keeper. And occasionally in this idyllic setting there are to be seen the children of the local villages. Tiny, earthy brown figures with closely cropped dark hair play in the dusty and unmade paths of the village streets. Four wheel bogeys, piled high with tiny human bodies, are their main source of entertainment. But whatever games they play, these children have not lost the art of amusing themselves.

This fertile land of Western Turkey is the land of the stooping figure. Everywhere is to be seen the body bent in the propagation of the growing crops. Outwardly the scene has not changed much in 2,000 years. Are we in the west any happier than these simple country people, who tend the land so that the land in its turn might provide them with the basic necessities of life? Catching only a fleeting glimpse of these folk as the coach speeds us on to our next destination, it is difficult to imagine them suffering from nervous depression. Do they, I wonder?

EPHESUS At the end of all this journeying through the Turkish countryside and the philosophising that has accompanied it, we have now arrived in the city of Ephesus, looking from a distance like some gigantic Cecil B. de Mille film set. This great city was founded by Athenian colonists in 1100 BC and it was once ''the first and greatest metropolis of Asia''. It was in Ephesus that the mother Goddess Artemis was worshipped and around her an elaborate cult of idol worship was devised which was ultimately to come into conflict with the Christian faith through the preaching of St. Paul. Today Ephesus is one of the most impressive and extensive ancient city sites in the whole of the Hellenistic world, and it does not require a great leap of the imagination to picture oneself in the company of the rich merchants and silversmiths of this city as they traversed the Arcadian Way.

I thought of Ephesus as some partly concealed ruin standing remotely in the Ionian countryside with precious little remaining, but this is far from the case. View the great facade which housed the library of Celsus or the Baths of Scholasticia. Better still, stand in the theatre which once seated 24,000 spectators and reflect on the riot that took place there when Demetrius and his fellow silversmiths vented their anger on St. Paul for undermining their lucrative temple trade by preaching worship of the one true God. Ephesus comes alive. Christianity itself comes alive and the famous XIX Chapter of the Acts of the Apostles takes on a new and a fresh meaning.

April 18th (Wednesday) DELOS

In a pre-visit lecture on Delos we were informed that the main feature of the island was its light. It is probable that from the word 'Delos' we derived our word 'psychedelic'— meaning shining light. But there is precious little of the light of Delos as we set out for the island on this chilly April morning. We looked more Viking people than Mediterranean, as we stepped ashore in three layers of warm clothing. Delos in mythology was the home of Apollo. The island was once a holy place, lying central in the Cyclades and the half-way point on the journey between mainland Greece and Ionia. The island is tiny; the visitor can comfortably walk around it in a day. Now it is unhinhabited but because of its vast ruins and importance in the ancient world, Delos is visited regularly and still has an air of mystery about it. The island was festooned with Spring wild flowers; a lovely sight.

MYKONOS We have now arrived at an island called Mykonos—not far from Delos—which according to the guide books has nothing very historic to commend it. That in itself makes it unusual. We are told ''in classical Greek history Mykonos played no notable part''—so there we are, that's that. Then why are we here? For no other reason, (one suspects) than to spend our Greek drachmas in the many tourist shops that are lying in wait for us. The business of holiday shopping troubles the brain of the tourist, and the mind isn't at rest till the task of carrying home useless junk, which nobody wants, has been achieved. Bits of china, fake urns, leather wallets, polka dot skirts, cutouts of Greek houses in plaster of Paris, imitation frescoes, hats, caps, shoes—it's all bought and trundled around and shoved at the back of cupboards when home is reached. We are all at it, the world over, and what would our economies do without it.

We therefore spend our shopping hours in Mykonos, looking for things to fit other people's feet and the day reaches a pitch of frantic frustration when we try to find something we can buy for our junior son, Richard. The idea of footwear of some sort comes to mind. Now his feet are so large than any shoes we buy him resemble oil rigs. They are of such proportions as to be perfectly suitable for sitting on the sea bed. He is sixteen and takes size twelve in shoes, so that is the problem a very obliging Greek shopowner is up against when she tries to sell us a pair of pretty leather sandals. Mary attempts to work from a map of his feet she has brought with her. Eventually we end up buying him an oil lamp. We have the same trouble when it comes to buying our eldest son something. He has strange feet also. As his head is smaller than his feet, we settle on a cap!

April 19th (Thursday) ATHENS

It was in Athens that I suffered my first bout of severe cultural indigestion. I was alright going up to the Acropolis, sliding and slipping with the other thousands of sightseers on the marble ascent to the Parthenon. It was when we had to descend and somebody mentioned 'museums' that I finally rebelled. The prospect of traipsing around yet another museum in the company of steaming plastic raincoats proved too much, and I stayed put in the coach whilst the others went off to do their stint. As the driver left the bus, after sealing the vehicle up with me alone inside, I realised what it must be like for a child left by its careless parents in a motor car in the heat of the midday sun, with the windows shut. For a moment I thought pedestrains passing by were thinking a similar fate had befallen me and were about to come to my rescue with pick-axe handles, but eventually they went their way, leaving me alone.

In isolation I watched the whole of modern Athens pass before my eyes. How entertaining and thoroughly uncultural it all was: there, for instance, a fellow whose job it was to strip posters off lamp posts; here a lady doing roaring trade selling peanuts from a barrow; confusion caused by trolley buses, separated from overhead wires. A modern city was on the move, and as remote from that ancient city on the hill as was possible to imagine.

One feature of ancient Athens, however, that did impress me more than anything was the sight of the Temple of

44

Theseion which can be seen from the Acropolis, tucked away to the North-West side of the Agora on the plain. This lovely temple is the best preserved classical building in Greece, the reason for its preservation being in part due to its constant use; first as a temple to Athena, then as a Christian church (dedicated to Saint George); its roof was restored as late as the 14th Century AD. Now once again it stands as a ruin, forever part of Ancient Greece. What new religion will man think up in another 2,000 years' time?

20th April (Good Friday) CORINTH

During the night this homely old ship of ours has journeyed from Athens to New Corinth, passing once again through the Corinth Canal. Soon we will be on our way home, calling in on Corfu and parts of Yugoslavia before we reach Venice. But this morning we have taken the short coach ride from New to Old Corinth. What can be said about the ancient site of Corinth? Well, very little that hasn't already been stated— but I cannot let the opportunity go by without mention of a feeling that has haunted me ever since we set foot in the antique world. That is the overwhelming sense of the harmony of these ancient sites within their natural sur- roundings; it is as if the countryside and ruins, by the passage of time, have been fused into a unity. Nothing is discordant, not a single ruined temple sits awkwardly on its foundation. This conception of the man-made in harmony with nature has pre-occupied painters through the ages. It was one reason why, when the master English watercolourist painted the picturesque, his composition included temple ruins to give balance to the scene. And as we looked out upon the ruins of Corinth, there again was this over-riding impression but this time with one important exception. Truly the eyes focussed on that now familiar sight. The Agora, the Temple of Apollo, the Sacred Spring, the ancient pavement by the side of which stood the ruined shops—but outside that framework there were other things going on in Corinth. For instance, if the eyes and ears didn't deceive, over the garden wall were the sights and sounds of the 20th Century. Houses with the familiar television masts and down the road, no more than 400 yards away, shops selling meat and butter and cheese; children playing in nearby streets. So in one sense Old Corinth is not some remote site, far removed from the commerce of the 20th Century, but adjacent to the here and now.

21st April (Saturday) CORFU

Today we were let loose in Corfu to do exactly as we pleased. Last night we had a lecture on ''Corfu Ancient and Modern''. All that historical stuff went by the board as we trotted off into the town, looking more like children just let out of school than culture vultures. With not an ancient ruin in sight, we acted in a wholly irresponsible way—sitting down doing nothing, buying cakes or just standing and staring with hands in pockets, watching the island's patron saint, St. Spirito, being trundled around the town to the accompaniment of massed bands and youth marching in step. It was St. Spirito's Day. It was teacher's rest day too and, by golly, we were making the most of it. The visit came to a crashing finale, literally crashing, because this was the very day when Corfucians (or whatever they call themselves) go to pot—yes, to pot. On the stroke of eleven clay pots, thousands of them, are hurled from balcony windows into the squares below. It is part of the Easter celebrations, and a pretty mess of the place they make.

22nd April (Sunday) YUGOSLAVIA

We are nearing home. They have just instructed us to put our watches and clocks back one hour. We must also be in Communist country because our cruise people are getting worked up over the passports.

On our way to Yugoslavia we gawped from the safety of the ship's rail at the mystery land of Albania and have wondered

46

why on earth people cannot get into or out of the place. It looked quite normal from where we stood.

Today we have spent the first of our two days in Yugoslavia —at a little island (and town) called Korcula, in the Adriatic, half-way between Split to the North and Dubrovnik to the South. Korcula appeared to be a sleeping town lying in wait for the summer visitors. The pretty houses seemed uninhabited, the shops and cafes were closed. I have rarely experienced anything quite like this except in a Swiss skiing resort out of season.

Before our arrival at Korcula we had to divert to Dubrovnik to land two sick passengers who had been ailing on board ship for some days. The lady was suffering from pneumonia and the gentleman a suspected heart attack. It was Easter Sunday in Dubrovnik, which gave us the opportunity of witnessing in a Communist country the Easter celebrations of the Serbian Orthodox Church. The churches were crowded and there was a good sprinkling of young people among the worshippers.

23rd April (Monday) SPLIT

I detect a certain weariness as we make our last port of call; this time it is the city of Split in Yugoslavia, built by the Emperor Diocletian at the beginning of the fourth century (and so on and so on). I think we have all had enough of gazing at ruins. There comes a time when the brain will absorb no more. Still we go through the motions of trying to appreciate the ancient city of Split. It was not for the lack of trying on the part of our young Yugoslav guide. She was one of the best we have had. In fact all our local guides have been excellent—all but for one male in Turkey, who harangued us on the splendours of Turkish carpets to such an extent that the entire party took a dislike to him. I am sure he must have been a shareholder in the local carpet factory. The best Greek guide we had—she stayed with us on board ship during the entire time the vessel was in Greek waters—was Zoe. She was a middle-aged lady who was so proud of her Greek history that she

47

became carried away. Her eyes would flash and she would raise her arms to heaven in a paeon of praise to the gods. She was the Maria Callas of the Swan Hellenic Line.

24th April (Tuesday) VENICE

And so it is back to Venice from where we commenced this trip two weeks ago. By contrast with our departure, Venice was kind to us with its weather. The sun shone and there was an Easter Carnival atmosphere in the air. And Swans fulfilled their promise right down to the last detail to look after our every needs (they even asked if I would like an electric wheel chair at Venice airport). How glad they must have been to see the back of us—well not exactly us but cruise 231. It hasn't gone at all well for them ever since we set sail from Venice a fortnight ago. There were the storms of the first two days involving picking up seamen in distress and delayed arrival times with much re-arranging. Then there were the strikes of the museum staff on the mainland which meant a hastily re-arranged itinerary. Sick people had to be cared for, and eventually landed outside the normal schedule. The jinx even followed us back to Venice. It was with us in the tiny water bus that conveyed us from the city to the airport. A lad sitting up front was having a nose bleed. The propellor of the boat kept scraping the bottom of the lagoon. We made it—but only just. As we disappeared out of sight of the cruise director, we noticed, to our horror and then wry amusement, one of the wheels falling off a wheelchair as it was being trundled across the runway of Venice Airport to join Cruise No. 232. Surely Swan Hellenic deserve better luck than that!

HOME TO HAY

28th April (Saturday)

Well, here we are revived, refreshed and returned from the Antique World of Greece and safely restored to the antique world of Hay. It is nice to be back. Everything is very much the same as we left it. The house next door is still un-occupied, our much-planned patio garden at the rear is crying out to be completed and the gallery for some of the time has been manned and has brought in money. But, most importantly of all, the "Limited" is still operating, and that is good to see.

Now we are about to enter into the slow, silent month of May, which consistently is a poor time of the year for sales. It is punctuated by a couple of false starts caused by the introduction of those most un-British of Bank holidays, May Day and the Spring Bank Holiday. On these days Hay is full of visitors, which always arouses a feeling of false optimism, because the impression is created that this is the start of the holiday season. But it is nothing of the sort. The visitors leave for home, and Hay is left waiting for their return again in Mid-June. From a sales point of view Bank holidays are a waste of effort. They have become a time for providing somewhere for the visitors to roam and mooch; often with bored and disgruntled children; achieving little in the way of sales. In other words all we provide is a service for the general public. This doesn't surprise me in the least; as tourists we used to inflict the same indifference on our equivalents every time the ship berthed at some tourist spot in Greece. Often on the arrival of our cruiser the local shops would optimistically open their doors under the mistaken impression that we were about to unload surplus drachmas for their goodies. How disappointed they must have been when we returned to the ship emptyhanded.

Greg, at the Cinema Bookshop, complained bitterly last August Bank Holiday of having to clean up after two children who had been ill over his floor. The ice-cream seller down the road was the real culprit for this mishap. He probably makes more money than we who sell a more cultivated commodity. So it is now batten down the hatches and hang on until mid June.

May 4th (Friday)

I have always regarded our gallery as a meeting place where book and picture lovers, and indeed anyone who has anything worthwhile to say can come in and have a friendly talk. Some would argue that too much of this goes on, but I am proud that the gallery is the rendezvous of like minds, and over the years many new friends have been made this way. I provided a similar sort of venue this afternoon when an elderly gentleman walked in who seemed to be grateful for the opportunity merely to have a chat. He turned out to be an itinerant traveller who had visited many parts of the world in an old van that he both lived and slept in and was now looking for somewhere to park overnight. I directed him to the municipal car park after dark. Our car park in Hay offers one of the most spectacular views of the Black Mountains in the whole of the area. It amazes me how this wonderful site came to be chosen to perform such a mundane function. I last caught sight of him heading in this direction driving his mobile home up Castle Street.

Late in the afternoon Mary and I received an invitation from Peter Smith to take afternoon tea with him in his flat this coming Sunday. Mary accepted, provided we had cucumber sandwiches. I hope he realises she is only joking.

May 5th (Saturday)

I did think Hay was as far removed from the outrages of the 20th Century as one could possibly get, and certainly safe from such horrors as assassination attempts and bomb scares. But for one horrible moment last night I thought all that had caught up with us. The rumour was rife that the bridge over the River Wye at the Three Cocks had been closed and that all through traffic was being diverted via Glasbury because of a bomb scare. Just think of it. This is the very bridge we pass over every time we come to Hay, and we could have been blown to smithereens. Apparently men had been seen acting in a suspicious manner and appeared to be planting something (a bomb?) under the bridge. Panic stations. But it all turned out to be a false alarm; the men seen operating in a somewhat sinister way were in fact planting clues under the bridge for a car treasure hunt to be held next day!

This morning two young dealers from Hamburg came into the gallery asking for books on unusual sexual practices and anything by Havelock Ellis. I had a quick glance at our "Wonders of Nature" series and the "Pastimes and hobbies" section but could not find anything that interested them.

In case the reader should wonder what has happened to all my friends at the Blue Boar, let me hasten to assure them that we were re-united this Saturday evening and that Jim I and II were in place but Jim III was not present. The winter hearth fires have now been extinguished by Chris, and so too was the pub conversation which seemed strangely muted.

May 6th (Sunday)

Today we took afternoon tea with Peter Smith, elegantly served from a porcelain tea service. He must have taken Mary quite seriously for there were the cucumber sandwiches, surgically treated to dispense with the crusts. These tiny, delicate morsels had been made suitable for the genteel and toothless. Peter beforehand had done a very fine mathematical calculation to see how many of these postage stamps would be needed and he had worked out exactly eight sandwiches per person. But on a final count it was discovered that I had had nine to every one else's eight, which threw our host into confusion. Nobody was able to give an accurate explanation as to what had actually happened. But clearly old Grabbing-Fingers was somewhere to blame for the discrepancy, and eventually we were able to calm him down. All this scoffing and checking of figures and done to the accompaniment of an old recording of "The Importance of Being Earnest" with Lady Bracknell and her cucumber sandwiches, so we were in very good company. Besides which, I understand English afternoon tea is coming into fashion again. If they can do this sort of thing in the Ritz, why not in Hay?

May 17th (Thursday)

I am a "Friend of the Royal Academy". This means that for the payment of an annual subscription I have free admission

51

to the various exhibitions that are held in Burlington House throughout the year, the use of the reference library, the members' private coffee room, and, most prestigiously of all, an invite to the Private Pre-view of the Annual Summer Show. This is not to be confused with the very Private Pre-view, reserved for God and various other luminaries. But still an invite to the Private Pre-view is honour enough, and an event to be planned and eagerly anticipated. In fact the word "honour" was used by the President of The Royal Academy in his invitation. It said quite plainly—The President of the Royal Academy requests "the honour of your company". Immediately visions sprang to mind of this particular "friend" standing nonchalantly leaning on umbrella survey-ing the nation's talent as they did in Turner's day. What thoughts of cultural exclusiveness! And so it was that we set out with high expectations on the Rapide bus from Cardiff to London. Unfortunately 33,000 other "Friends of the Royal Academy" set out with exactly the same intention. By the time we reached the courtyard of the Academy the whole place resembled Wembly on cup final day. In fact I did witness scenes bordering on football hooliganism. For instance, a woman was propelled through the gallery's swing doors by a malicious youth at such speed that she made a free landing in the marbled floor foyer, and then proceeded to attack her assailant with her rolled-up umbrella. It could have turned into an ugly incident. The cloakroom was under seige from "friends" anxious to deposit their bombs, and the main carpeted staircase resembled an impressive crowd scene from Aida—with elephants! I cannot exactly recall walking into Gallery One under my own steam; rather I was carried in by the sheer weight of numbers, my feet never once touching the ground. Vast armies were on the move: when eventually the shoving and heaving paused in order for them to regain their own momentum, I was conscious of looking at pictures. They were all six feet above my head. What lay at eye level was quite impossible to tell; at a rough guess they could well have been paintings. And so the "honoured friends" continued to pour in until eventually we were able to move neither forwards, backwards nor sideways under our own initiative; only when the herd instinct asserted itself

52

were we able to move in any direction at all. By this time we were so encased in the throng that it looked as if we were all wearing neck braces. I trod on something—and found at my feet a perfectly formed midget. I dread to think what eventually could have been this dear person's fate. After a half hour we managed to escape to the comparative calm and tranquility of the Piccadilly traffic. It cost us dearly to recuperate our strength in an expensive coffee shop, but it was well worth it.

The alley that runs directly alongside the Royal Academy afforded much more pleasure. In this little side lane, modest book dealers erect canvas stalls and sell their treasures. With all the time in the world and ample space, I managed to purchase a rare and interesting Eric Gill item; such a change from the mad scramble taking place in the marbled halls not more than two hundred yards away.

May 20th (Saturday)

Books on pavements always fascinate the public and here we are this morning, in the town of books, putting them out on the window sills for an airing and, we hope, selling as well. Perhaps I ought to explain how this demeaning practice came about. A couple of years ago I was so fed up with the sight of books that had lain unwanted and forgotten on our shelves that in a fit of frustration I took it into my head to unload the lot on the nearest tip. "Steady on," said Mary as I was about to load them into the car, "why don't you put them out at 20p each?" So in they came and out they went again, priced at 20p. It worked. We are all on the look-out for the bargain. At the magic sign over they came to find the bargain. A gentleman said he had been looking for twenty years for one particular book, to which I responded, "Well, we've been looking twenty years for you." To tread on pieces of silver that have been dropped through the letter box when the gallery is closed is one of the joys of closing for lunch, in that the public's offerings do at least go some way to pay for the beer. Besides, it also serves two other very useful functions. It is one way of getting rid of unwanted stock and it tempts the

53

Putting out the 20p section

public to cross the road and sometimes to cross the threshold
as well.

May 21st (Sunday)

Book Fairs, Antique Fairs, Collectors Fairs, call them what
you will, are all the rage at the moment and not a week goes
by without some event of interest being put on in a part of the
country. There are, of course, fairs and fairs. Some command
an international reputation and are housed in the glittering
ball-rooms of prestigious hotels. At the other extreme there
are those modest village hall efforts which cater for no more
than the collector of bits and pieces: bric-a-brac. However
one may view them, and grand or modest as they may be,
they are certainly ways of increasing the cash flow, and have
the bonus of enticing the seller out of the claustrophobic
atmosphere of the bookshop, especially on lonely winter
days. To have a gossip or a grumble with one's fellow dealers
is in itself therapeutic. From the public's point of view it is
very convenient to find dealers assembled under one roof
instead of having to traipse around town to find them. I am a
great believer in fairs and am drawn to them by such simple
attractions as the smell of coffee brewing, the warm snug
atmosphere of stalls crowded together, creaking floorboards
and the sense of a common pursuit in search of a common
interest. It is in search of such kindred spirits that we have
taken to exhibiting at a small antique fair in Cowbridge these
past few months. We have gone to some trouble to hand pick
our wares, displaying Aldous Huxley, P. G. Wodehouse and
Evelyn Waugh first editions, with a sense of anticipation that
someone would appreciate them. But we have found ourselves in lonely isolation and treated with indifference by a
public who are hunting for other things. I must admit it has
come as something of a disappointment when we have seen
our books flicked through and turned over as if they were
cheap paperbacks. What is the point of it? There is no
common ground, nothing whatsoever that would spark off a
lively bookish conversation. I would prefer to sell a good

book at cost price to a genuine lover of books, rather than be ignored in this way.

I think therefore we must give the next one a miss and move on.

May 24th (Thursday)

A young man came into the gallery this morning asking if I would display a poster advertising a pottery exhibition he was putting on in Hay next month, which I did gladly. He said he nearly bought something from us two years ago!

In an earlier part of this diary, readers will recall the slight phobia I have developed over the possibility of being taken ill in the flat when I am alone, and of the difficulty that would then be encountered in contacting the outside world. I didn't realize what problems old people must encounter when they are in a similar situation and living alone. In our house in Hay, we have two very precipitous flights of stairs, and I remember a young doctor who was once staying with us fell down these stairs breaking her leg in the most complicated way. She lay there quite unable to call for help. Supposing the same thing happened to me: what on earth would I do? Suddenly I had an idea—a whistle—a whistle strategically placed at a spot on the stairs where I was most likely to land would be just the job. Rosie over the road was selling off whistles at £1 a time, and one of those would act as a very simple but efficient alarm system. I would need only to reach out from a lying position and just blow for help. The trouble was, I very nearly turned over on my ankle as I trod on the thing going down to the bathroom in the middle of the night and just prevented an accident. It is however going to be a boon. If only Frank had had one! Frank was one of our drinking companions up at the Blue Boar, who lived alone. One day Frank was found dead in the chair—with a whistle like mine he might have been alive today.

May 26th (Saturday)

The visitors are back in town and that quiet spell about which we have all been complaining recently has at last come to an end—at least until the Fall. During these past few weeks Hay has never been so quiet; it was as if the town was returning to the rural backwaters of yesteryear. But this Saturday evening there were signs that life of a sort was back, if the attendance at the Blue Boar was anything to go by. The three Jims were present, but the settle was also occupied by four teenagers who were complete strangers to us. They were playing some sort of alphabetical pop quiz which they were making up in their own private way. When the Zs and Frank Zapper had been reached, I introduced myself by enquiring who was winning and from that moment we all got on like a house on fire. I heard about Manchester, the drudgery of living in an environment where one township leads into another with no greenery in between, and of the problems of trying to fish in polluted canals. Hay to them, with its surrounding countryside, was heaven. As we parted they remarked how grateful they were that somebody had taken the trouble to talk to them. It was refreshing to chat to such honest-to-goodness natural young people.

May 27th (Sunday)

Time has been going on since Peter Smith had me around to try out his walnut dumplings. For the return match I had promised him a Lancashire Hotpot, but at the last minute I chickened out, and this afternoon came up with nothing more daring than braised steak, jacket potatoes and apricot tart. But he seemed to enjoy it and was all smiles afterwards.

May 28th (Bank Holiday Monday)

Today has been a typical Bank Holiday Monday in Hay—lots of visitors roaming about the place looking cold, hungry and bored and towing in their wake grizzling children on the verge of tantrums. We have had our fair share of them in the gallery as they have wandered around not knowing what they are about. One book shop owner has resolutely refused to have anything to do with it and has gone off to London. For all the takings, we could have done the same.

We have also had rather well dressed, spikily aggressive, middle-aged ladies who have come into the gallery offering to sell something or have made cheeky efforts to knock us down as if we were serfs. I find them rather tarsome.

And somebody else, *very* different.

"Golly, you did arf frighten me," said the little girl turning around to see who had tapped her on the shoulder. "Well," said the man standing behind her, "I was a bit worried because all the books you are carrying seem nearly to be as tall as you." "I was looking for books for me mum," said the little girl in between moments of blowing bubble gum, "because we are going home tomorrow." "And where are you from?" enquiried the tall man—"We come from Meriden," said Abigail (by this time she had told the man her name) "and Meriden is famous because it's the centre of England and I sing in St. Lawrence Church choir." "You come from Meriden?" said the man eagerly —"Meriden?—and you sing in the choir at St. Lawrence? Well now, I've just the thing for you." "What's that then?" said Abigail. And turning she and her pal Martin and the rest of the gang accompanying her trouped off behind this man to see what he had in his bookshop.

When they arrived at the stranger's shop, he brought out a really beautiful book which contained two watercolours of the very church which Abigail attended. Inside the book were inscribed in copper plate all the names of the people who worshipped at St. Lawrence Church back in 1913 and this book was presented to the vicar to mark his retirement.

The man wasn't very keen to let Abigail and her friends handle this beautiful book because he could see they had sticky fingers from the bubble gum but they all agreed it was a 'smashing' book. But the man did ask if they would do him one favour. "If I write a letter to your vicar," he said—"will you promise to hand it to him when you are in Church next

because I am going to offer this book to him and his Church?''
So off went Abigail and Martin and all the gang from
Meriden, goshing and gollying at this amazing find, and car-
rying the message with them.

I wonder; will I ever hear from the vicar of Meriden?

June 1st (Friday)

Hay has once again had its quota of media coverage. A couple
of weeks ago it was an article in the Reader's Digest which
brought the crowds flocking in. This week it has been an
item on radio's dear old Woman's Hour which has brought
them all back to have a squint at us. And the attention we are
receiving has to do with the business rivalry between Messrs.
Morelli and Booth. Richard Booth has found the going difficult recently and has had to retrench to the other end of town.
Leon Morelli has stepped in with his marketing ability. One
hopes there will be room for both of them in Hay; certainly
our wish is that Richard Booth should survive to fight
another day because we could do with eccentrics like him—
the world is fast running out of them.

June 5th (Tuesday)

My car, which for over two years has faithfully transported
me back and forth over the Brecon Beacons in all winds and
weathers so that I may make my weekly appearance in Hay,
has finally conveyed the message that things to do with its
innards are not quite what they should be, so this morning I
have taken it to the doctor's for an examination. Dr. Ford-
thorne diagnosed the trouble as something to do with a
rocker gasket (whatever that means) and while she is being
operated on, I have had a few spare hours to idle away in Cardiff. Where else could I have spent those hours except in a
second-hand bookshop in the city centre? Rummaging
around bookshops invariably means kneeling, stooping,
bending and reaching, which is never good for me. These

fairly innocuous movements once again led me to walk (when I left the shop) like a paraplegic. There is only one answer to this condition: to sit down on the nearest bench. So when I came out, clutching my few acquisitions, I had to find the nearest municipal resting place as soon as possible. I eventually found one in the pedestrian precinct in the shadow of Cardiff's Roman Catholic Cathedral, which also happens to be the haunt of the City's drunks, down and outs and drop-outs. It was in their company that I settled down behind the high walls of my bench, to mull over my newly acquired gains. After half an hour of quiet dossing, I looked up to discover my son Andrew passing by. Judging by our expressions I don't know who was the more surprised, father or son. He hesitated for a moment before acknowledging me, because he was with a friend. Surely his father hadn't fallen on such hard times since last he had seen him? But any rate there I was, and there he was. There was no way he could ignore the old man now. ''Hello,'' said he, looking down at me surrounded by brown paper bags, ''I thought you were a tramp but you can't be because you haven't a bottle of sherry with you.'' So off we went for a pint, none of us looking particularly elegant.

June 7th (Thursday)

Whether he got the idea from television the night before, when they showed all those D Day landing films, I shall never know, but Jim I was in a reminiscing mood up at the Blue Boar this evening. He said Jim II was working up at Tetbury and wouldn't be home until the week-end. With Jim II out of action, Jim I then proceeded to produce for me out of his inside coat pocket a series of faded sepia photographs of himself and his family. First there was Jim when he was two, then one when he was thirty-two, and finally a snap of him at sixty-two. There then followed shots of Jim's daughters and grand-children ending up with one of Jim's sons guarding the Queen Mother. It came to an abrupt halt with the arrival of a regular who eventually embroiled me in a somewhat hysterical conversation. Hysterical conversations are not uncommon at the Blue Boar. One such took place not so long ago between myself and a German visitor. He came from Cologne, he informed me, and was a physicist by profession. He had travelled from home, arriving at Edinburgh and making his way down through Newcastle, Nottingham and Leicester, finally ending up in London. From there, he said he went on to visit "Lourdes". Yes,—Lourdes. "Lourdes?" I queried, at a loss to understand why a German physicist should be on a pilgrimage to Lourdes. "You went to Lourdes?" "Ja," he replied in gaping astonishment—"Ja, Lourdes Vy?" Now, to my simple mind, a physicist journeying to Lourdes didn't quite match up and I questioned him further. "Are you Catholic?" I hesitatingly enquired. "No, vy should I be?" "Well—urgh—are you religious?" I persisted. "No!" he snapped, quite plainly at a loss to understand what on earth I was getting at. And then gradually the German mark dropped, as it suddenly dawned on him—"Ah, Lourdes," said he triumphantly, beaming all over his face, "NO NOT LOURDES—LORDS CRICKET GROUND!"

8th June (Friday)

The storm cones have been raised over Hay again. That is, the police "no parking" bollards have been placed all down the pavement outside the gallery. This is usually a sign that the gas man cometh or the electric man or the water man or any other man bent on causing chaos. And when they appear you can be sure Hay will soon be transformed into a First World War battle scene of Mons proportions. This time it is the turn of the paving men, who transform our paths into pretty jig-saw puzzles. At first I thought this intricate pavement motif was for the benefit of the disabled and their carriages but one sees the snakes-and-ladder effect everywhere, so I don't think it can be meant for this section of the community. Whatever it was in aid of, these men were about to start work on the opposite side of the road from our gallery. My heart sank. I have seen shops in the town besieged and

61

left isolated, as pavements have been ripped up; elderly ladies negotiating narrow planks and wobbling on splindly legs like tightrope walkers in an effort to get into a shop of their choosing. God forbid that this should happen to Arvona Gallery. People will risk life and limb to get a loaf of bread but surely not for a watercolour. I made my thoughts known to the foreman as he was about to wheel into position his Mulberry Harbour right outside the pretty Hay Wain shop but he didn't seem to understand me. I was told, on the side, that they have run out of jig saw pieces and there wouldn't be enough to reach down to Arvona Gallery. I hope he is right.

June 9th (Saturday)

We have just had a visit from a man, a clergyman at that, who is the only known person ever to have beaten down OXFAM on the price of a book! What about that?

Last January I reported on the demise of the cake shop across the road and of the lady the like of whose rhubarb tarts we shall never see again. Well, like a phoenix from the ashes has arisen something a good deal grander, known as the Lions Corner House because it stands foursquare on the corner of Lion Street. In the Corner House they serve Lasagne, Chilli Con Carne, Ravioli and Bananarama and things. They are shortly to apply for a licence to sell wines and spirits, which will be a blessing. At the moment we have to smuggle in (quite legally) a bottle of wine every time we have lunch, which is all rather sordid.

June 15th (Friday)

I have just decided to treat myself to a complete set of the Brontë novels—nothing more, nothing less—and I am about to embark on a good read. I overheard this event being relayed down the telephone by my junior son to his big brother, Andrew. "The old man's got Wuthering Heights," he shouted, as if I had something wrong with me.

62

June 18th (Monday)

This morning I allied myself to the Cowbridge Arts Class (advanced group) of which Mary is a member. I joined them on a trip to London to visit the Royal Academy Summer Exhibition. They went around in a good deal more civilised manner than when we went on the opening day. I do not belong to the class for the simple reason that I am terrified of having to show my dreadful daubings to anyone, including the tutor. I remember joining such a class three years ago and the deep embarrassment when anyone peered over my shoulder to see my efforts. I have a phobia of my work being seen or heard. It stems, I think, from an experience I had when I once went in for a piano competition. There were only two of us taking part. I got off to a bad start, playing the Beethoven piano sonata, opus 49 No. 1 when in point of fact I should have been playing the opus 49 No. 2. This straight away put the judges in a bad mood. By the end of the performance my nerves and theirs were in such tatters that my feet were as if glued to the pedals. As a result the instrument resembled nothing so much as an echo sounder. I came third! The same sort of terror comes over me when I publicly take up a paint brush. I stiffen with tension and it wouldn't take much to send me screaming into the night. So the trip to London was for no other reason than getting there on the cheap. I went off to Bertram Rotas in Long Acre. Half way there I became semi-paralysed with the heat of the London streets. It really was quite disabling and after Rotas I could no more attempt bookshops than fly. Leicester Square provided my first resting ground, followed by a long spell in Golden Square. So my trip was little more than a tour of a couple of London squares, but it wasn't a bad day out.

June 23rd (Saturday)

I went into the gallery this morning to be met by a deeply pungent, rancid smell. For one moment I thought we were going to be faced with the same problem that they have had up in the Cinema Bookshop: mice decomposing under the

63

floor. Imagine my relief therefore to discover that it was only an old carton of skimmed milk going off. I soon put paid to that. Skimmed milk, Flora margarine instead of good old butter, the extraction of fat from this and that—Lord help us, they are taking the joy out of everything these days. I am surprised our skimmed milk had even the strength to go off.

Hay, except for the muted call of the young female town crier today, is a quiet place. Last night in the Blue Boar, at one point in the clock's motion there were only three of us on the premises, and neither Jim I, II or III were present—which puts one under a heavy obligation to make conversation. This is not Hay of old. What has become of the place?

This afternoon has been ever so slightly enlivened by the presence in the gallery of a stranger who examined, handled and mulled over an expensive bird book before reaching a decision to purchase. Even then the finance to complete the deal seemed to come in instalments. The gentleman appeared to be producing money from every conceivable part of his anatomy. Hands were plunged deep down into trouser pockets; the insides of coats were turned out, money came down his sleeves or was found nestling in turn-ups. Anyone looking at us from outside must have thought I was carrying out a body search. So frantic was the quest for finance that at one point in the proceedings I thought he was going to take all his clothes off. The only thing lacking was a bleeping instrument such as they employ at air ports to suss out concealed metal objects. The search came to a temporary halt at £16. We still had another £7 to go. So off he went again, fumbling into various parts of his clothing. At last a treasure trove of paper and silver money lay heaped on the table in front of us, and we were able to call the search off. He has a nice book there, and I am sure he has earned the time to read it.

EPILOGUE

The schools have broken up for the Summer holidays, and for the umpteenth year in succession children are being traipsed around the town's bookshops. The old familiar sights and sounds are back with us again. Coaches full of visitors are lined up in serried ranks in the most spectacularly scenic car park in all Wales. Bronzed bodies, in between getting in the self catering groceries from this shop and that, flit in and out of bookshops. And, like some Tuscan village, the locals and Summer visitors stand in groups on street corners exchanging gossip. Occasionally the cry of disbelief echoes from the town's grey stone walls as yet another bookshop is discovered and the complaint goes up—"This place seems to be full of old books." In our gallery, too, already we have had the season's blight of grubby fingers as prints have been mulled over. Windows have had to be wiped clean of greasy noses pressed up against glass to see what we are about.

Then a day in September will arrive and suddenly, overnight, they will be gone, and Hay will once more decline into solemn slumber until the following Spring. It is knowing what to do in these silent and tedious months of late Autumn, Winter and now early Spring that worries me most. There was a time when book dealers from all over the country and further afield would sustain the town and keep it interesting through these sparse and barren months, for there were always rich pickings to be had. Not so now. The time when holiday-makers were an added bonus has gone. We have come to rely on them for our very livelihood, for the Continental book-dealers are few and far between. The more inquisitively bookish who come are here because they have read in the press or seen us on television. Unless we have something really worthwhile to offer in the book line, Hay is by default, going to be living on its past glories, and cannot last for very long like that.

When these visitors arrive in Hay what do they find? They certainly find a town set in the most beautiful countryside. Nothing can take that away; not even the passage of time erodes its superb location, for the River Wye, still skirts the town, and the Black Mountains and Hay Bluff stand guard.

Despite all this, however, I have a feeling of unease; there is something missing. What is it? I think it has to do with the characters who have gone from this town recently. We no longer have dear Chalky White, who operated from his tiny, dank, coal-heated bookshop, selling from mittened hands as he heated his drop of soup over a stove. Or Malcolm Lindsay, the most gifted bookseller I have known, who sold "his treasures" from living quarters in the old morgue or, farther back still, Alfie Ward visiting us in the gallery with tales of folklore, bartering his netsinkers for old prints and knocking back whiskies out of tea-cups, or Bill Preece laughing his head off at he knew not what cycling his way home. All these eccentrics have gone, leaving the self-styled "King of Hay" (to whom this town owes much) in quietude and semi-exile. But the King is still in his castle; I wonder if and when he will reign again?

I think opportunities have also been missed to really establish Hay as a cultural centre. It surprises me that no-one in the town has hit upon the idea of organizing conferences and seminars akin to the book trade which in combination with holidays might well have attracted visitors from all over the world to this beautiful area. Hay could, with imagination, have been transormed into the Glyndebourne of the book world. Instead, it has gone for the gimmicks and in the process become something of a joke. I make these remarks conscious that I have not made any contribution to the idea either. I have to plead distance as the factor which prevents me taking an active role in such ventures.

As the eccentrics have gone, so too has a lot of the fun departed with them. Will we ever see repeated the quaint sight of books being loaded into pony and trap (probably for the benefit of some unsuspecting camera crew from abroad, who have been beguiled into thinking that this is an everyday sight) or a fellow bookseller, literally staggering up Castle Street, bent under the weight of six folio volumes of Ruskin's Modern Painters, or books being rescued from incineration to be resold next day at a profit? What has become of the man who claims to have run all the way from Cardiff to Hay backwards?!

For ten years, both in Winter and Summer, these events and characters have called me back to Hay. It has been worth travelling these thousands of miles from my home in the Vale of Glamorgan, if only to share in the life of this unique place. As I close this diary, the town is crowded with Summer visitors and there is life all around. What will happen when they have gone and the mists of Autumn fall and we are left in solitary isolation and to our own devices? It is then that one's loyalty to Hay will truly be put to the test.

BUT WAIT, THERE IS HOPE FOR US YET. Little Abigail and Martin and the rest of the gang from Meriden, the centre of England, have been true and sturdy messengers of the Word. Today, this 21st day of July, the roll of honour, dedicated in 1913 to the retiring vicar of St. Lawrence Church, Meriden, by his faithful parishioners, has in 1984, been carried back with much love and affection, to the place where it rightly belongs.

LONG LIVE MERIDEN, LONG LIVE HAY.